KNOW YOUR CHRIS[illegible]IANS

CW01619053

By the same author:

Pilgrim's Programme

The Plain Man Looks at Himself

Him We Declare (with Bishop Bardsley)

Onward Christian Soldier (biography of S. Baring Gould)

Fisher of Lambeth (biography of Archbishop Fisher)

Woodbine Willie (biography of G.A. Studdert Kennedy)

Odd Man Out (biography of Lord Soper)

British Police in a Changing Society

A Time to Die

No Other Gods

Pilgrim's England

The Christian in Retirement

Martyrs of Our Time

Seekers and Finders (with Kate Purcell)

Evidence for the Holy Spirit

Comfort and Hope

Also in Know Your Christians series

- Ten Missionary Pioneers
- Ten Witnesses for God
- Ten Spiritual Leaders

KNOW YOUR CHRISTIANS

Ten Social Reformers

by

WILLIAM PURCELL
Canon Emeritus of Worcester

MOWBRAY
LONDON & OXFORD

Copyright © William Purcell 1987

First published 1987
by A.R. Mowbray & Co. Ltd,
Saint Thomas House, Becket Street,
Oxford, OX1 1SJ.

All rights reserved. No part of this publication may be reproduced, stored in a retrieval system, or transmitted, in any form or by any means, electronic, mechanical, photocopying, recording, or otherwise, without the prior permission in writing from the publisher, A.R. Mowbray & Co. Ltd.

Typeset by Comersgate Art Studios Ltd, 52 St Clements Street,
Oxford OX4 1AG.
Printed in Great Britain by Cox and Wyman Ltd., Reading.

British Library Cataloguing in Publication Data

Purcell, William
Ten social reformers.—(Know your Christians).
1. Social reformers—Biography
2. Christian biography
I. Title II. Series
362′.922 HN13

ISBN 0-264-67130-9

CONTENTS

INTRODUCTION

From time to time down the centuries some Christian men and women are called upon to make a particular impact on the history of their time. These are the social reformers, who, by their devotion to a cause and leadership of it, change the shape of society. William Wilberforce in the eighteenth and nineteenth centuries did this in the case of the slave-trade. This infamous traffic in human beings had been for years accepted as normal; but Wilberforce, through a life-long struggle, managed to bring about its abolition. Around the same time Hannah More, moved by the poverty of the people in her native Somerset, set in train a programme of action which enormously improved the quality of their lives. And so it was with Elizabeth Fry, who moved by the terrible conditions of women in prison, set out to improve their lot. Similarly, it was the condition of factory workers in Victorian England which moved Lord Shaftesbury to the many reforms which he set in train. And so it was also with Josephine Butler, who, disturbed by the depraved conditions of prostitutes on the streets of London, was stirred to do something about the sexual exploitation of women. All these were inspired by their Christian faith. That was the root and ground of all that they were and all that they did. But this is not yesterday's tale; the contemporary scene has also witnessed those who, as social reformers, have been, and are equally, active. Such are Donald Soper the Christian pacifist, Group Captain Cheshire with his Cheshire homes, Cicely Saunders with her hospices for the dying, and Martin Luther King with his message of liberation to the Blacks, which did so much to bring them towards an equality of citizenship in the United States.

WILLIAM WILBERFORCE

(1759–1833)

'A little man, as thin as a shadow, drawing one side of his body after him, as if paralytic, hurried across the floor with a brisk, tottering step . . . and said in substance, that schools in Ireland were most desirable and should be organized by all means'. This was Wilberforce, as seen by a contemporary in the House of Commons in 1811. Frail and worn with unresting activity, Wilberforce may have been, yet his magnificent eloquence – lively, witty and always spontaneous, moved the hearts of all who heard him. Truly, his frailty belied his multifarious activities, as he turned tirelessly from one moral and religious project to another, organizing and directing with relentless pressure. There was no month when he was not engaged on evangelical matters: the Bible Society; the Church Missionary Society; the Proclamation Society Against Vice and Immorality; the School Society; the Sunday School Society and, above all, the abolition of the slave-trade, which established him as the nation's leading christian philanthropist.

Wilberforce's life began conventionally enough. His parents died when he was a boy and he was educated by a wealthy guardian and later, on the death of his grandfather, became a wealthy man himself. He trod the usual path for one of his social status: three years at St John's College, Cambridge, then elected in 1780 as Member of Parliament for Hull, at a cost of eight thousand pounds.

In London he became a close friend of William Pitt and embarked on a life of dining, gambling and opera-going. However, while on a trip to the continent in 1784, with a friend who happened to be an evangelical, Wilberforce was, as he said, 'much affected in conversing with him.' Overcome with remorse, he wrote in his diary for October 1785, 'the deep guilt and black ingratitude of my past life forced itself upon me in the strangest colours, and I condemned myself for having wasted my precious time, and opportunities and talents.'

He returned to Parliament in the spring of 1786 as a converted christian. Looking with new eyes on the moral scene around him he declared that, 'God has set before me as my object, the reformation of manners.' The first moral institution he set up was 'the Society to Effect the Enforcement of His Majesty's Proclamation against Vice and Immorality' (1788), known as 'The Proclamation Society'. At the time of its beginning this society was considered to be a tool of national reform, but, in fact, it was probably more valuable for its use as a proselytizing agency, a uniting force which gave other evangelical people a coherent purpose and activity. It was the first of a network of institutions organized for charitable, moral or religious purposes and may be seen as the beginning of the evangelical crusade.

As well as this, Wilberforce was making all possible use of his parliamentary position and his friendship with the Prime Minister. Soon he found himself the leader of a small group, nearly all Tory, but on moral issues belonging to no party but the evangelicals. This group became known as 'Wilberforce's neutral party' or 'the Saints' and numbered, by 1820, about thirty members.

Undoubtedly the greatest moral crusade which Wilberforce, aided by 'the Saints', led, was the fight to end the slave-trade – 'that odious traffic in human flesh', as Wilberforce once described slavery as early as 1773. British trade depended heavily on slave traffic, so intense opposition arose when the Abolition Committtee was set up in 1787. Wilberforce and his evangelical friends spread information about slavery throughout the country, and soon thousands and thousands of determined men and women had enlisted their support for the Abolition Act. Year after year the Act was introduced to Parliament and rejected: pressure had to be kept up for twenty years before the slave-trade was finally abolished in 1807. However, Wilberforce had to wait a further twenty-six years before he heard, on his death-bed, that slaves had been emancipated within the British Empire itself.

The battle for the Abolition Act established Wilberforce as the leader of the evangelical movement. During the fight to abolish slavery, having made himself a household name, he felt the time had come for a public confession of his religious belief, and in 1797 appeared his *Practical View of the Religious System of Professed Christians Contrasted with Real Christianity*. His aims in writing this were twofold. Firstly, he wanted to improve conditions for the working classes and to bring their condition to the attention of the wealthy; and secondly, he was aware, of course, of the conflict in the Church between the controlling orthodox group and the small evangelical body. Wilberforce, as the leader of the evangelical movement, addressed in their defence a powerful upper class who would not listen to a mere clergyman: he realized that the evangelical attempt to reform a nation was certain to fail unless they won over a substantial number of the ruling class, who to a great extent set the moral tone of the people.

Wilberforce set out in his book the principle of evangelical Christianity: he commented on the growing prosperity of the age contrasted with the increasing decline of religion, manners and morals. He reminded the rich of their duties to the poor and urged them to turn away from their 'nominal' Christianity to the real Christianity to be found in personal commitment. The book was an enormous success and seven and a half thousand copies were sold in six months. 'What a phenomenon', wrote John Newton, 'has Mr Wilberforce sent abroad. Such a book by such a man, and at such a time.'

Not only was the book a success in terms of sales, but its exhortations were influential, and the 'reformation of manners' which Wilberforce had campaigned for took place gradually before his eyes. The old upper classes, together with the newly-wealthy, became more concerned with their social responsibilities and, by the beginning of the nineteenth century, some of the coarseness and cruelty characteristic of the previous century had disappeared.

This climate of social change made it easier for Wilberforce and his evangelical circle to extend their network of benevolent societies which spread and multiplied, so that between 1788, and Wilberforce's death in 1833, about four hundred societies and hospitals had been conceived, among which the 'Climbing Boy's Society' was one of the most useful. Its attempt to rescue chimney-sweepers' apprentices from barbarous treatment attracted the support of both non-evangelical and evangelical people, including Lord Shaftesbury, who was still trying to achieve the Society's stated aim fifty years after its inauguration.

The seed from which the other societies grew was undoutedly the 'Stranger's Friend Society', founded in 1785 by the methodists, and reorganised by the evangelicals in 1802. The object of the society was, says the Report for 1806, to 'seek out and relieve those who, from sickness, want of employment, or unforeseen and unexpected calamity, are experiencing the greatest distress or literally perishing from want; and secondly to endeavour . . . to cause the voice of Providence to be heard in the afflictive dispensation'. This definition could accurately describe the main aim of most of the other benevolent societies.

Yet Wilberforce's reform of the nation needed a kind of catalyst which would arouse the passionate devotion of men and women, as the Abolition Act had done before; a cause which could inspire and put into action religious zeal, which could carry the evangelical campaign further than benevolent societies or hospitals could ever hope to do. That crusade was the extension of the 'British and Foreign Bible Society'. Founded by Wilberforce and other influential members of the Clapham Sect in 1804, the 'Bible Society' seemed to many to carry with it 'the zeal and charity of the apostolic age', as Bishop Porteus' chaplain noticed. It was, perhaps, the supreme evangelical testimony, and became immediately popular as thousands of men and women, grateful for a project that offered active service in the christian cause, came forward to help with promoting, translating, printing and distributing the Bible or parts of it, in one hundred and forty languages and dialects, including fifty-five in which it had never before been printed. By 1825 its operations extended throughout the British dominions.

Another far-reaching project which Wilberforce promoted, was the expansion of the 'Church Missionary Society'. His biographer records his statement that to further the Christianizing of India was an even more important mission than to bring liberty to African slaves. This he endeavoured to do, although his amendment to the East India Company's charter, providing for the 'religious and moral improvement' of the natives in British India, was defeated in 1793. Still, Wilberforce was able, through the Missionary Society, to promote the cause of missionaries; to be their parliamentary sponsor.

Wilberforce, long before the end of his life, had achieved a unique social and political eminence. He had done this by leading the evangelicals and others to attempt a heroic task – heroic because of its impossibility – to reform the manners and morals of society. Perhaps he may best be described in his own words, from *Practical Christianity*, as a man who 'will studiously and diligently use any degree of worldly credit he may enjoy, in removing or lessening prejudices: in conciliating good-will and thereby making way for the less obstructed progress of truth.' He died on 29 July 1833 and parliamentary business was suspended – an unequalled mark of public approbation – for members to attend his funeral; the funeral of a man who had never held office yet had been the voice of his age: the incarnation of a national conscience.

HANNAH MORE

(1745–1833)

'It is a singular privilege to have a *consecrated* pen and to be able and willing to devote our talents to the cause of God and religion', wrote the Reverend John Newton to Hannah More in 1787, shortly before the publication of her first manifesto. For Hannah More, by then famous for her dramatic tragedies, *Percy* (1777) and *Fatal Falsehood* (1779), and describd by Dr Johnson as 'the most powerful versificatrix', the world of theatre and fashion was fading away into triviality as she became drawn into a circle of leading evangelicals. Soon she withdrew from London to a country house in the Mendips called Cowslip Green, 'which place I hope', she wrote, 'will favour my escape from the world generally.' Shortly after her move she published her first manifesto, *Thoughts on the Importance of the Manners of the Great to General Society* (1788), and so began, at the age of forty-three, a vigorous outpouring of manifestos and tracts which were to make her a revered spokesman for morality and religion.

Hannah More was born in Gloucestershire, her parents being what the eighteenth century called 'of humble stock' – it is possible that her father was a domestic servant at Stoke House, Gloucester. The eldest of the sisters, sent to a Bristol school, she taught the others and soon, with the aid of a subscription, the sisters were able to set up a boarding-school for young ladies in Bristol.

As a child, Hannah had shown an aptitude both for writing and for piety: 'In her days of infancy, when she could possess herself of a scrap of paper, her delight was to scribble on it some essay or poem, with some well-directed moral', states her biographer. At seventeen years of age she embarked on her career as an author by producing a pastoral drama called *The Search for Happiness*, which has been described as 'a work of a virtuous tendency suitable for the young', (*Fathers of the Victoriana*, Ford K. Brown). Perhaps because of the popularity of this play, Hannah More retired from the Bristol school and went to London in 1775, where she mixed with the great of London society – Dr Johnson, Burke, Garrick and Sir Joshua Reynolds. However, when her circle of friends widened to include William Wilberforce and other evangelicals, she realized where her inclinations lay.

Retreating from London to Cowslip Green, she began her life of usefulness to the evangelical cause. Her first statement, *Thoughts on the Importance of the Manners of the Great to General Society* (1788), was designed to strike at the source of impiety, the upper classes. If the spirit of religion was to operate on the people, it must act first on 'their superiors, it must be received into the heart and exhibited in the life of the rich and great', proclaimed Hannah. The manifesto's motto was, 'You are the makers of morals': it was a preliminary statement, an opening address to a careless ruling class. Hannah's second manifesto, *An Estimate of Religion of the Fashionable World* (1791), was longer and sharper in tone. It struck particularly at the belief, commonly held by the fashionable world, that the generosity of their charities and benevolences to the poor exempted them from exhibiting true Christian virtue, 'to visit the fatherless and motherless in their affliction and to keep (themselves) unspotted from the world', as Hannah said. Benevolences are virtuous, she preached, only because of the christian love in which they are performed: the mere act of helping the distressed is not enough.

Hannah's sincerity was made evident by her plain, but passionate, tone, and the manifestos were well-received by the evangelical world: 'I was charmed and edified with it,' wrote Bishop Portens – Bishop of London – of the first manifesto, 'and am impatient to see it in the hands of every man and woman of condition in London and Westminster.' But her sincerity and her wish to be useful were shown on a larger scale by her establishment of a system of schools for her ignorant and impoverished neighbours in Somerset. In August 1789 William Wilberforce, while staying with the More sisters, advised Hannah that 'something must be done for Cheddar'. Although the cliffs were very fine, 'the poverty and distress of the people was dreadful'. Acting on this observation Hannah and Miss Patty, the youngest of the sisters, established a school at Cheddar and, in the course of ten years, had extended it into a system of schools for children, young people and adults. The main aim of the schools was to teach the pupils to read so that they might read the Bible: the inscription under the first stone of the school built at Nailsea stated that the building was to benefit the parish in its most important interest, that of providing education in the knowledge and practice of the christian religion.

It was her knowledge of the poor people of Somerset which led Bishop Porteus to ask Hannah to take up her pen to stem what he saw as the tide of evil – new philosophical ideas of freedom and equality – which began to pour across the Channel from 1790 on. Hannah, thought the bishop could provide a great service to the nation by providing some form of cheap literature which would urge piety, subordination and contentment on the masses. Hannah's first pamphlet, entitled *Village Politics, by Will Chip*, was extremely successful and was sold or given away throughout Britain. '*Village Politics* is universally extolled', Porteus wrote; 'it has been read and greatly admired at Windsor, and its fame is spreading rapidly over all parts of the United Kingdom . . . it is a masterpiece of its kind.' The pamphlet was the first of a long series which established Hannah as the world's leading practitioner in this kind of art. Hannah's aim was both to stress the dangerous nature of radical French philosophy and to assure the English working class that their conditions were good, or if not perfect, then to be borne stoically: 'Duties are fixed . . . laws are settled . . . a Christian can't pick and choose', (*Village Politics*).

Porteus approved Hannah's work and encouraged her to continue writing, suggesting that she produce three tracts a month similar to *Village Politics* – that is, loyal, religious pieces. These were sold by hawkers for a penny or halfpenny. Called 'Cheap Repositary Tracts', they were in enormous demand and, in 1795, one of Hannah's publishers stated that 'a million will have been sold before the end of next month. No such sale has ever been heard of in the annals of England'.

It was, without doubt, not the cheapness of the tracts but Hannah's racy, vigorous and simple style which made them so popular. Hannah knew her audience and so knew how to communicate with them. Her good and bad characters are immediately identified; the moral is pointed out by visible results: Black Giles falls while thieving and is killed (*Black Giles the Poacher, Continuing some account of a Family who had rather live by their Wits than their Work*); James Stock, honest and pious, rises to affluence while his fellow-apprentice, idle Jack Brown, sinks lower and lower, haunts evil resorts, goes to fairs and, at last, is ruined (*The Two Shoemakers*).

Hannah's straightforward honesty, her unhesitating statement of what she believed to be true, and her clear-sighted pointing-out of sin; 'Sin is the great cause and source of every existing evil; we should always prefer suffering to sin' (John

Newton), won her many admirers. By the time the 'Cheap Repository Tracts' were discontinued (1798), because it was believed that the flood of French radical ideas has ceased, Hannah's home in Somerset had become a place where earnest people came from far and wide to meet the celebrated christian woman.

But Hannah More's vigorous and remarkable life was not without its battles. The worst of these, which came to be known as 'the Blagdon Controversy', literally began as a parochial affair when the curate of Hannah's own parish, Blagdon, accused the adult school-teacher there, a Mr Young, of 'methodistical practices', and called on Hannah to remove him. Instead of defusing the issue by transferring Mr Young elsewhere, Hannah retained him and called in her influential evangelical friends – William Wilberforce, Bishop Porteus and others – to back her up. The curate, Thomas Bere, stood firm, and drew onto his side the leading men of the parish who were opposed to the 'dangerous' education of their labourers. The affair grew to be a more than local scandal when, on 12 November 1800, Bere gave public evidence against Young, and Hannah, perhaps in retaliation or perhaps because she wished to conciliate Bere, closed the schools. But the matter did not end here. Hannah's friends in London accused Bere of being anti-trinitarian and his bishop asked him to resign. He refused and, publishing instead a pamphlet stating his case, went to London to seek support.

The controversy, having spread to London, developed into a bitter feud between evangelicals and 'regular' churchmen. 'Such horrid reports are abroad,' Miss Patty wrote, 'that some strong measures must be taken, and that immediately. The emissaries of Satan are spreading strange things in London.' Eventually the affair died down: Mr Young was transferred to Ireland, Bere retained his parish and the schools reopened in all parishes but Blagdon. Hannah's final statement on the controversy is contained in a letter written in 1808; 'it showed me the vanity of human applause, and has led me, I hope, to be *more* anxious about the motives of my actions and less anxious about their consequences.'

At the age of fifty-seven years, Hannah left Somerset and moved to Barley Wood near London, where she was able to become closely connected with the Clapham Sect. This was an informal group of wealthy evangelical anglicans, and was so named because the majority of its members lived near Clapham and worshipped at the parish church. Among the most outstanding were William Wilberforce, J. Venn – rector of Clapham from 1792–1813, James Stephen, Lord Teignmouth and Zachary Macauley. Most of the sect, especially Wilberforce, had been known to Hannah before her move to Barley Wood, and she had shared for a long time the sect's keen sense of moral responsibility and the belief that religion should be manifested in good works. In that sense, she had been a member of the

Clapham sect ever since her early period in London.

Hannah's life at Barley Wood with her sisters has been described by a visitor thus: 'Surely there never was such a house, so full of intellect and piety and active benevolence.' Hannah continued to show an active interest in schools and to write works of more solidity than her 'Cheap Repositories'. These, especially *Practical Piety* (1811), were successful, and sometimes sold out on the day of publication. Soon she could say, modestly, that the only remarkable thing about her as an author was that she had written eleven volumes after the age of sixty.

Throughout her long life, Hannah had shared with many evangelicals a passion for 'the death bed scene': 'I know of nothing so interesting as the closing scenes of a champion of righteousness', she wrote to a friend. Her own last years were spent in relative contentment, although one unhappy event occurred. Living alone in Barley Wood since the death of her sisters, Hannah had become increasingly feeble in health and, in order that she might live her last days in peace, was prepared to tolerate her servants robbing her, as well as their drunken behaviour. Evangelical friends, however, persuaded her that if she condoned such behaviour she could be thought of as a 'patroness of vice', so the old lady was forced to leave her home and move to Clifton at the age of eighty-three.

Here she remained until her death, proudly showing her works – now translated into forty languages – to her many visitors. She died on 7 September

1833, aware to the end of the bond of humanity between her and the poor of Somerset.

ELIZABETH FRY

(1780–1845)

'We long to burn her alive', wrote the Reverend Sydney Smith in 1821 of Elizabeth Fry. 'Examples of living virtue disturb our repose and give birth to distressing comparisons.' Elizabeth Fry's daunting purity tended to chill even those of her own family: she pursued an ideal of perfection which was so remote from the concerns of most men and women that they could only mock or deride her, yet, by the time of her death, her passionate concern for good had touched people's hearts, and from her example flowed a wave of tolerance and compassion which swept through nineteenth-century Europe.

Elizabeth Gurney was born on 21 May 1780 in a dignified building, the Court House, standing back from the street in the centre of Norwich. Her father owned a wool-stapling and spinning factory nearby and was prosperous and well-respected, though his membership of the Society of Friends meant that he was unable to hold civil office. Elizabeth was brought up a Quaker; a nervous child who, said her mother, 'cried when she was looked at.' In spite of the fact that Elizabeth's mother gave birth to twelve children, she nevertheless had time to supervise their education, which was very advanced for the time and included, besides practical skills, such subjects as Latin, French, geography and 'the simple beauties of mathematics'. Girls as well as boys studied this curriculum, since Quakers believed that men and women were equal in the sight of God.

Sadly, when Elizabeth was thirteen her mother died, and from then on Elizabeth was periodically plunged into fits of frightening depression. These depressions would hang oppressively over the house, isolating her from the rest of the family; 'Dearest Betsy! she seems to have no-one for her friend; for none of us are intimate with her', wrote one of her sisters. Certainly Elizabeth, with her constant pangs of self-criticism and self-doubt, seemed out of place in the carefree and charming family: they enjoyed life and, unlike plain Quakers of the day, the children attended dances and dinners: 'I am,' wrote Elizabeth, 'a dissipated, idle, contemptible fine lady.'

However, a visitor to the quaker meeting house in Norwich – an American called William Savery – inspired the impressionable eighteen year-old so much that she persuaded her easy-going father to allow her to follow Savery to London, so that she might again hear him preach. Before long she recorded in her journal that, 'I shall always love religion through him but must always love it away from him'; and she prayed to grow more and more virtuous, to 'follow the path I should go in and not to fear to acknowledge the God whom I worship.'

Returning home, she struggled to maintain this

exalted attitude and consequently became more separate than ever from the rest of the family. She began to develop a life of her own, visiting the sick, reading to a little boy from the village and giving her clothes to the poor. Alienated from her pleasure-loving family, she found a friend in a shy young man called Joseph Fry, who soon fell passionately in love with Elizabeth and proposed to her several times. At last she accepted, though with some misgivings; 'I felt very changeable towards him, either like or dislike.' The couple were married on 19 August 1800.

By marrying Joseph she was able to live as a plain Friend, without the constant strain she had felt with her family. She became her own mistress, free to follow her own destiny.

At first, marriage proved difficult. The couple moved to the City of London and lived 'over the house' in Mildred's Court, with the Fry's warehouse for tea, coffee and spices on one side of the large house and the counting-house on the ground floor. Several clerks occupied the house and, when she moved in, Elizabeth found confusion everywhere. The life of a wife and mother – by the time she was twenty-four she already had three children under five – frustrated her: '. . . it does appear to me as if I might become the careworn and oppressed mother . . . may sink under the duties of a young mother and particularly young mothers like myself and my constitution appears to be delicate.'

However, her circumstances changed when John Fry's father left his house and estate at Pleshet to the young couple. The move suited Elizabeth and she revelled in the role of lady of the manor. As well as this, she came to realize her gift for public speaking. At meetings of the Friends she felt: 'like a bottle that has been corked up and pressed down and now there is an opening inside, there is much to run out.' In March 1811, she was formally acknowledged as a quaker minister and immediately embarked on the first of many visiting activities, travelling two hundred miles in two weeks to speak at meetings, sometimes experiencing an unusual state of ecstasy while she did so. She always spoke simply and to the point, and exerted such power over her audience that they came away stunned. For a woman to speak so publicly and so eloquently caused a sensation: 'God is no respecter of persons', observed a man present at one of her meetings.

In London for the winter, Elizabeth finally found a cause to which she could give herself wholly. A French Quaker visiting London, brought to her attention the horrors of Newgate prison; Newgate, renowned for its hanging days. Outside the debtors' door until 1790 women had been hanged and then burnt on piles of faggots while the crowd howled and shrieked. By 1813 they were hanged on the scaffold. The executions took place at eight o'clock on Monday morning and all the night before the crowd would assemble - pickpockets and their girls swaggering about the narrow streets, drunkards lurching from taverns in Newgate Street - while workmen built the scaffold, hung with black. A seat at one of the windows overlooking the gallows could cost up to ten pounds. Inside the prison the inmates lived in terrible squalor, the women occupying two long rooms and sleeping in three tiers – one row of bodies on the floor, the rest in hammocks in two tiers – without any bedding. On hearing of these appalling conditions, Elizabeth persuaded the governor to let her visit the women. This he was reluctant to do, saying that the prisoners were an unruly and desperate set who would attack her. This did not deter Elizabeth, however, who swept him aside and entered to find nearly three hundred women in the two rooms, some sentenced to death, some untried; young girls, old ladies and babies; cooking, eating, fighting. Here Elizabeth spoke and her audience listened as if hypnotised, to her eloquent voice, with its message of hope and love. Her mission had begun.

At first she concerned herself with the plight of the children, setting up a school for them in 1817. She and her helpers visited the prison nearly every day, bearing bibles, sewing materials and food for the prisoners. At first Elizabeth kept her experiment at Newgate a secret, but when she reflected on the despair and depravity around her she determined on a course that could not be kept quiet: 'Until I make some attempt in the plans for the women, I shall not feel easy' she wrote. After a lot of opposition she succeeded in persuading the governor to allow her to try to introduce cleanliness, religion and instruction into the lives of the female prisoners. In 1817, after the meeting with the governor, Elizabeth wrote, 'I hope I am not undertaking too much, but it is a little like being in the whirlwind . . . may I not be hurt in it.'

One of her first undertakings was to enlist the prisoners' co-operation; her insistence on this was extremely enlightened for her time. She drew up a list of rules, each one voted on separately by a show of hands. She appointed a matron, replaced rags with dresses and introduced the idea of paid employment; 'We may instruct as we will, but if we allow them their time and they have nothing to do, they naturally must return to their evil passions.' A visitor to Newgate soon reported that, 'I was conducted by a decently dressed person to the doors of a ward where at the head of a table sat a lady belonging to the Society of Friends. She was reading aloud to about sixteen women prisoners who were engaged in needlework . . . each wore a clean looking apron and bib. They all rose on my entrance, curtsied respectfully, and then, at a signal resumed their seats and employment.'

Elizabeth never reconciled herself to the death penalty. The more she saw of it – and she visited male and female prisoners and their families in the condemned cell and stayed to be with them to the last – the more convinced she grew that capital punishment was evil and produced evil results. Criminals could be sent to the gallows at that time for over two hundred offences, sometimes as minor as stealing a pair of stockings or forging a banknote. By using her unique position, Elizabeth began to direct public attention to the horror of hanging; but she was unsuccessful in saving the life of one of her favourite prisoners, Harriet Skelton, who was hung for passing forged banknotes under the influence of her husband. Elizabeth's unsuccessful plea to the Home Secretary to spare Harriet only succeeded in annoying him, but this blunder taught her that she must tread with care; her position was unique but it was also vulnerable.

Elizabeth's next task was to improve the conditions on ships used for transportation. Realizing that she could not alter the prisoners' sentences, she believed that at least she could make the parting easier for them. Instead of being loaded into an open cart, clapped in irons and followed by a jeering crowd who pelted them with stones all the way to the river, she organized transport in closed carriages. Bringing up the rear of the convoy in her own carriage was Elizabeth herself, carrying her bible and the box of tracts which she took everywhere with her. Elizabeth reorganized the cramped conditions on board and divided the women up into classes of twelve, based on the Newgate system. She classified them according to their age and the nature of their crime and set aside a small space for a schoolroom for the children. The last time Elizabeth boarded the convict ship *The Maria* before she sailed, she stood on deck and read from her bible in a clear voice to the assembled prisoners, while sailors climbed high into the rigging to get a view of the strange scene below.

As Elizabeth became well known, she travelled throughout Britain advising on prison improvement. She journeyed abroad, too, as her fame spread, and became an international novelty, inspecting prisons and making recommendations, while crowds gathered, bringing gifts to her carriage and begging for tracts. Her travels became triumphant progresses and her life can indeed be seen as a triumph in itself. From a sheltered background and a lack of formal training, she had won herself a place of honour in courts and governments the world over. Determined to use her talents to some purpose, she had battled with her nervous disposition and had become a courageous innovator. Perhaps her main achievement was to acknowledge the humanity of the prisoners and to consider them as individuals with individual human needs.

Elizabeth died on 13 October 1845, a delicate old lady who had borne eleven children, managed a family estate and looked after a weak husband. She will be remembered for her gift of touching peoples' hearts by her own deep religious feelings and by her passionate concern for good.

LORD SHAFTESBURY

(1801–1885)

Some say that Shaftesbury's philanthropic career may be traced from the time when, as a young boy, he witnessed a pauper funeral. As he turned a corner on one of the streets of London, he came upon a group of drunken men carrying a rough coffin of the kind only used for paupers. Reeling, they lurched from side to side, one of them stumbled and the coffin fell to the ground. The degrading scene affected Ashley deeply, though it would probably be an exaggeration to say that the event changed his life. Why Ashley, seventh Lord Shaftesbury, spent his life campaigning for the destitute will probably remain an enigma. 'I feel', he once said, 'that my business lies in the gutter, and I have not the least intention to get out of it.'

Ashley's ancestry, parentage and upbringing in no way indicated his future development. His parents were harsh, remote figures in his life, summoning him and his brothers and sisters for inspection rarely, and leaving them to the care of servants and school-teachers. Ashley spent a wretched childhood both at home and at school: 'I think there never was such a wicked school before or since, he wrote in later life; 'The place was bad, wicked, filthy; and the treatment was starvation and cruelty'. Some respite from his childhood misery was offered by the affectionate housekeeper, Maria Millis, who described herself as 'most truely your affectionate friend'. She told him bible stories, taught him a prayer and showed him the realities of christian love, which must have contrasted strangely with the disciplined church-going which was part of his school and home life. When she died she left him her gold watch which Ashley always wore in later life, saying, 'This belonged to the best friend I ever had.'

The story of Ashley's life until his marriage is one of a search for love and support. Unable to win any sign of paternal feeling from his father, he wrote sadly, 'his natural tendency is to avoid me and all his children; he has refused them a home . . . He commanded me to leave his house in London, and will receive me nowhere else.' After gaining a First at Oxford, his formal entry into public life came in the autumn of 1826, when he entered the House of Commons as Tory member for Woodstock. But during his early adult years it was not politics but a desire to get married which occupied his thoughts and energies. While visiting Vienna, he fell in love with Antoinette von Leykham, who, lovely and desirable though she was, came from a socially unacceptable home – her father, a baron, had married an opera singer, their house was full of odd characters and they were not received in Viennese society. 'Liebe, dear Liebe', Ashley wrote, 'was and is an angel, but she was surrounded by, and would have brought with her, a halo of hell.' He was persuaded by influential friends not to marry her. Affectionate, passionate, impressionable, Ashley persevered in his search for a wife, recording in his diary; 'Methinks that if I could find the creature I have invented I should love her with a tenderness and truth unprecedented in the history of wedlock.' Eventually, he found her. Lady Emily Cowper, or Minny, as he came to call her, was 'lovely, accomplished, clever, ladylike, of modest demeanor, with an air of virgin indifference towards all admirers.' Although there was a snag – her mother's family were ardent Whigs – this did not deter Ashley and in 1830 they were married.

Starved of domestic life in his childhood, Ashley sought to steep himself in family affairs. He was, and always remained, an affectionate husband and father. He and Minny had ten children whom he watched over with tender vigilance. It is as though he wished to make his home a model of his universal ideal. Certainly, the principal motive behind his philanthropic work was to minimize the sufferings of children and to maximize their chances of a secure family life. It provides an insight into Ashley's complex character to reflect on his own insecure childhood and compare it with the security he wished for others.

Now established with a happy family base, Ashley could devote his passionate energies to poverty and destitution in all its forms. He turned his attention first to the condition of the inmates of the White House at Bethnal Green. These 'lunatics', as they were then termed, were confined in crib-rooms; that is, rooms containing nothing but bedsteads filled with straw. Often chained up, they were treated as malefactors, beaten, starved and handled with brutality. Respectable society treated mental illness as something disgraceful and unnatural, and this attitude Ashley attempted to change, having himself an intuitive understanding of these mentally-ill outcasts. His speeches commending their condition were among his most eloquent; '. . . we must not run away with the notion that even the hopelessly mad are dead to all capacity or moral exertion – quite the reverse; their feelings, too, are painfully alive', he told the House on 23 July 1844.

In June 1845 he introduced a group of bills establishing a 'Lunacy Commission' whose powers were to inspect all licensed asylums at least twice a year and, at the same time, insuring that an adequate living standard and more compassionate treatment was offered. Ashley reminded the House that they were, in a sense, legislating for sane as well as insane society: 'The most exalted intellects, the noblest affections, are transformed into fatuity and corruption, and leave nothing but the sad though salutary lesson – how frail is the tenure by which we hold all that is precious and dignified in human nature.' These bills were amongst the most important passed by Shaftesbury since they were instrumental in altering the public's attitude towards mental illness, though many remained bigoted in their superstitious attitude towards the treatment of the insane.

Although Shaftesbury spent all his philanthropic

life – nearly sixty years-campaigning for 'lunatics', it is for his work with destitute children that he is better known. 'Wastrel children', as he often called them, were a product of the new cities spawned by the Industrial Revolution. Growing rapidly, cities sprouted new houses while empty spaces were filled with whatever buildings offered the quickest profit. Tenements, gin-palaces and warehouses abounded and, because the rent was so high, housing conditions became more and more crowded and squalid. The very-poor would be crammed into 'rookeries' – large houses converted into warrens of one or two-room dwellings. In these noisy, fould-smelling fire-traps crime was endemic. It was easy to slide down the poverty scale into these slums; the only alternative being the workhouse, prison or transportation.

Shaftesbury had been appointed by Parliament as adviser on child welfare in 1832 and he made it his business to acquaint himself with the squalid side of city life. He made several visits to lodging-houses and described them in an article he wrote to the *Quarterly Review* in 1847 in some detail: in one room was to be found 'besides children, sixty adults, a goodly company of males and females of every profession of fraud and violence, with a very few poor and industrious labourers . . .' He was also taken by Dr Barnado to see the conditions of homeless children and found a group of them sheltering at night under a tarpaulin. Dr Barnado estimated that, in the late 1870s, there were about thirty thousand destitute children roaming the London streets.

Shaftesbury, appalled by what he had seen, devoted himself to rescuing poor people from two circumstances over which they had no control; bad living conditions and bad employment. This meant that the spectrum of his concern covered poverty and destitution in all its forms and particularly centred on London, where poverty's cause and effect were, perhaps, displayed at their worst. He acted first to improve working conditions in factories, particularly for children, stating that, 'I confess that my desire and ambition [is] to bring all the labouring children of this empire within the reach and opportunities of education – within the sphere of happy useful citizens.' Although Shaftesbury was instrumental in reforming conditions in factories, it was left to a contemporary to pass the Ten Hour Act in 1847, which limited child-labour in factories to ten hours a day. Ashley, meanwhile, became the parliamentary champion of the 'Ragged Schools Union', later called the 'Shaftesbury Society', run by the London City Mission. The purpose of this union, founded in 1844, was to rescue children before they became part of the criminal population, as well as having the religious aim of saving their souls. Besides this, Shaftesbury devoted himself to the cause of children chimney-sweeps – 'climbing-boys' – and, after a long battle to improve their wretched and dangerous conditions of work, and the death of several climbing-boys from suffocation in the chimneys, finally passed an Act in 1875 ensuring that no more boys were sent up chimneys.

From these initial reforms others proliferated. Refuges were established for destitute people of all ages; work was found for them, sometimes on training ships such as the *Chichester* or the *Arethusa*, sometimes by setting up institutions to which they could belong, such as the Shoe-Blacks Brigades or an Industrial School and sometimes by enabling emigration to Canada or Australia. This philanthropic mission to the underworld spread the influence of Shaftesbury. He was at the heart of the reform of the cities: the 'patron saint of the poor and oppressed'.

But Shaftesbury's mission to alleviate human suffering spread wider. He, amongst other early public-health reformers, such as Chadwick, realized that the quality of life depended, to a large extent, on the quality of housing. Having seen for himself the degrading slums in which the poor of London lived, Shaftesbury was determined to fight private landlords, superstition, ignorance – all the barriers which stood in the way of reform. In 1848 he became President of the General Board of Health and worked with Chadwick and others to lay the foundations of the British public health system. The Board of Health established a network of local health authorities; it showed how cholera could be beaten; it provided a back-up service of expert knowledge. Throughout his period of presidency, Shaftesbury used his personal authority and influence to administer the board and to pass reformative acts through parliament: the two most important being the Lodging-Houses Act (1851) which placed lodging-houses under the control of local authorities, and a Permissive Act, enabling local authorities to build their own model lodging-houses. He could therefore be said to have introduced the principle of 'council-housing'.

To the end Shaftesbury continued to personify the personal ideals of the Victorian age. Surviving his beloved Minny by several years, he eventually died peacefully at the age of eighty-four. His memorial service at Westminster Abbey testified to his position as figurehead of the poor. Crowds came from nearly two hundred organizations whom he had represented and a statue was erected in his honour by Gladstone. This statue – the statue of Eros in Piccadilly Circus, London–reads as follows: 'Erected by public subscription to Anthony Ashley Cooper K.G. seventh Earl of Shaftesbury, born April 28th 1801, died October 1st, 1885. During a public life of half a century he devoted the influence of his station, the strong sympathies of his heart, and the great powers of his mind, to honouring God by serving his fellow men. An example to his order, a blessing to his people, and a name to be by them ever gratefully remembered.'

JOSEPHINE BUTLER

(1828–1906)

Liverpool Cathedral contains a memorial window to a woman who, until recently, was in danger of being forgotten. The reason for her obscurity is simple: she cared for the rights of destitute prostitutes and women with venereal disease. As she herself said, 'It is such a dirty, vile, unclean subject that we are afraid to touch it, and yet other women bear it.' The cause of these 'other women' became her cause, and for this she is remembered both by Liverpool, where she lived for many years, and by the Church of England Calendar of Saintly Worthies, where her death – 30 December 1906 – is remembered with these words: 'Social Reformer, Wife, Mother.'

As a girl, Josephine and her sister Harriet were known as 'the belles of Northumberland'. They and her other brothers and sisters – Josephine was one of a large family – had a happy childhood, galloping too fast to hounds and enjoying an unusual amount of freedom. Most particularly they were encouraged to discuss all kinds of social problems amongst themselves, their father being very involved in reforms, particularly the abolition of slavery. Josephine's mother was a devout evangelical and from her may have come Josephine's religious intensity.

As a young woman Josephine experienced a vision. She recorded it thus: 'I heard a wailing cry somewhere among the trees in the twilight which was deepening into night. It was a woman's cry – a woman aspiring to heaven and dragged back to hell – and my heart was pierced with pain . . . I longed to leap from the window and flee with her to some place of refuge . . . I cannot explain the nature of the impression which remains with me to this day but, beyond that twilight, and even in the midst of that pitiful cry, there seemed to dawn a ray of light and to sound a note not wholly of despair.'

In 1852 Josephine married George Butler and went to live in Oxford where he was a University Examiner. Here she continued to feel drawn to the particular sufferings of women, noticing the prejudice, common everywhere and perhaps especially common amongst celibate Oxford dons, against 'impure' women. 'A moral lapse in a woman', Josephine noted, 'was spoken of as an immensely worse thing than in a man . . . A pure woman, it was reiterated, should be absolutely ignorant of a certain class of evils, albeit those evils bore with murderous cruelty on other women.'

Moving to Cheltenham in 1857, the Butlers and their four children enjoyed a happy family life. However, a horrible tragedy occurred. One evening, as the parents returned home from a drive, their only daughter, Eva, rushed to the upstairs landing to greet them, leant too far over the bannisters and fell to her death on the stone floor below. 'Never can I lose that memory', wrote Josephine, 'the fall, the sudden cry and then the silence . . . Would to God that I had died that death for her.' After Eva's death, Josephine was never really well again, consulting nine doctors in four years about her heart and feeling breathless at night. However, the tragic death had another effect on Josephine's development: 'I became possessed with an irresistible desire to go forth and find some keener pain than my own . . . I had no clear idea beyond that . . . my sole wish was to plunge into the heart of some human misery, and to say to afflicted people, 'I understand. I, too, have suffered.'

In 1865, George Butler became Principal of Liverpool College. As Josephine remarked, 'It was not difficult to find misery in Liverpool'. The seaport, a recipient of enormous wealth, contained some of Britain's most squalid slums where half-starved Irish, who had fled the potato famine, lived as best they might. Orphans lived abandoned amongst the debris of Liverpool's Dockland and in foul-smelling cellars lodged Liverpool's derilicts – women and children, many of them prostitutes. The age of consent, in those days, was twelve years, and one and a half thousand prostitutes were under the age of fifteen.

Josephine visited the inmates of Brownlow Hill Workhouse, where she must have presented an astonishing vision. As she recorded: 'I was taken into an immense, gloomy vault, filled with women and girls – more than two hundred at that time. I sat on the floor among them and picked oakum. They laughed at me and told me my fingers were of no use for that work, which was true. But while we laughed, we became friends.' She began, with her husband's support, to take the worst cases into her home so that she could look after them.

Soon the Butlers had established a house nearby as a refuge for destitute women. They were much criticized for this, especially George who, some believed, should have prevented his wife from acting in so rash a manner. However, this home acted only as a stop-gap. Josephine was concerned with the lack of employment for women and the fact 'that prostitution is caused not by female depravity or male licentiousness, but simply by underpaying, undervaluing and overworking women so shamefully that the poorest of them are forced to resort to prostitution to keep body and soul together.' Josephine came to believe in women's emancipation. Every woman, she stated, had four rights: the right to be educated, the right to earn, the right to exercise the vote and the right to own the money she earned. She became a prominent petitioner for women's suffrage and was appointed President of the North of England Council for the Higher Education of Women. Inevitably she became involved in the cross-fire of controversy between reactionary males, and females, and suffragettes, like herself. For it was still a commonly-held belief that a woman's place was strictly in the home and that there ought never to be occupations for women outside it.

This commonly-held belief, however, did nothing to mitigate the circumstances of the two-and-a-half million homeless women who, in 1868, had to either starve or become prostitutes. Moreover, prostitution had entered a degrading new phase since it became legalized or 'regulated' in 1864. The passing of the Contagious Diseases Act in that year, and its renewal in 1866 and 1869, meant that licensed prostitutes were attached to one of eleven towns which had been endowed with a state brothel. The prostitutes were examined at regular intervals in an effort to check the spread of venereal disease. But, worse than this, special police were instructed to arrest any woman or girl in the listed towns who was suspected of being a prostitute. She would undergo a compulsory medical examination and, if she refused, could be sentenced to hard labour. She had no appeal against a corrupt and powerful police force. Horrible mistakes were made. One girl was found to be a virgin, but not before she had been forced into a straitjacket and her legs held apart with metal clamps while the examination took place. Other women committed suicide after being wrongfully arrested. Josephine became determined to alter the situation, 'If women had possessed the franchise', she wrote, 'the Contagious Diseases Acts could not have been passed.'

Josephine became the founder and president of the Ladies' Association for the Repeal of the C.D. Acts, which was launched in 1869. Her manifesto, published in a national paper, set out the Association's objections to the Acts, which included its objection to the abolition of the civil rights of women; and its objection to the condoning of vice, and the double standard whereby it was acceptable for a man to give vent to his natural feelings by using prostitutes. As well as this, Josephine travelled, in that year, nearly three thousand miles, speaking against the C.D. Acts, and also published the first of her thirty-eight pamphlets and thirty-six books. Throughout her campaign, she felt a spiritual inspiration or 'call' to carry on: the centrality of the presence of Christ and, as she felt, his abiding presence with her, should not be forgotten.

As her campaign grew in fame and importance it was used in political elections, Josephine being asked to speak on behalf of the 'women question' and therefore against the Liberal Government who were eager to quell the whole issue. On one occasion, in Pontefract, Josephine had to jump to safety when a stable loft in which she was speaking was set on fire; on another she had to hide behind the counter of a grocer's shop to escape an angry mob.

Meanwhile she had become a powerful figure, and her cause could no longer be ignored. Parliament set up a Royal Commission to enquire into the workings of the C.D. Acts, and Josephine was asked to give evidence. In spite of her pleas and lucid argument, the report stated that; 'There is no comparison to be made between prostitutes and the men who consort with them. With one sex the offence is committed as a matter of gain, with the other it is an irregular indulgence of a natural impulse.'

Josephine persevered, however, carrying her personal crusade abroad to visit St Lazare, the prison hospital for vagabond women. Here she found such terrible conditions that she could only say, 'My heart was ready to faint within me'. She decided to try to prevent conditions in England from ever becoming as appalling as those in St Lazare, and founded the International Federation for Abolition, based in Geneva, and supported by powerful political figures. She and her colleagues discovered impressive new evidence of corruption. In Liège, Belgium, waggon-loads of children were brought from all over Europe. Children, some as young as eleven and twelve, were bought or abducted, and beaten if they refused to co-operate or tried to run away. Josephine's allegations were indignantly refuted, but she repeated her accusations on oath and stressed that where there were no state brothels there was no slave-traffic; where there were state brothels there was an active market.

Public opinion began to change, and the Government was again forced to re-examine the C.D. Acts. Josephine was again asked to give evidence, and this time was able to relate her continental discoveries. Public opinion continued to turn in her favour. At the opening of Parliament on 28 February 1883, a first attempt to introduce abolition into the debate was ignored, but the people of England no longer ignored the facts that Josephine had for so long been setting before them. The matter was again raised in Parliament in June 1883 and this time the Acts were suspended by a sizeable majority. 'Say unto Jerusalem, that her warfare is accomplished', exclaimed Josephine as the result was announced.

Although the Contagious Diseases Acts were no longer in operation, Josephine still had a point to prove. The evils of brothels and slave-traffic needed to be brought even more to the attention of the public. She and her son, George, visited London brothels and published their findings in the *Pall Mall Gazette* under the title 'The Maiden Tribute to Modern Babylon'. There is no need for anyone to press upon me the reality of Hell . . . for I have been in Hell', she commented. The Acts were finally repealed in March 1886. But Josephine's work was not yet over and she continued to fight for the rights of women, particularly prostitutes, until the end of her life. As well as this, she devoted much time to writing about her husband, who had died in 1890. He had always supported her in all her endeavours and had, eventually, to resign from Liverpool College because his wife's activities were becoming too controversial. She wrote *Recollections of George Butler* 'to show . . . that he was even more to me in later life than a wise and noble supporter and helper in the work which may be called especially my own. . .' She died, a fragile and beautiful old lady, aged seventy-eight. All her life she had fought, believing that, however impossible the cause, 'God and one woman make a majority'.

WILSON CARLILE

(1847–1942)

In later life Wilson Carlile would often assert that 'Joey Billy' played a large part in the formation of the Church Army. 'Joey Billy' was a wooden doll that the young Wilson had played with until the arms, legs and hair had been lost. This stump of a doll, wearing only an old red flannel petticoat, became, in its battered old age, Wilson's favourite toy. 'How dear Joey Billy was to me', Wilson Carlile once said; 'There was so little left of him that he was rather difficult to nurse, so I used to tie a string round his neck and swing him round my head, to express all I felt about him . . . Joey Billy was the real founder of the Church Army. He taught me to love poor broken, disreputable things, and it is for men and women in that state that the Church Army exists.'

Born in London, the son of a prosperous business man, Wilson spent much time at home during his childhood as he suffered from a spinal weakness. This weakness meant that he could not play games and was often ill; but his enforced time at home was not spent idly. It was during these early years that Wilson developed two gifts which were to prove useful to him in later life; his ability to play the trombone and piano, and his business acumen. When Wilson was seven years old his father gave him a little account book and made him a weekly allowance of a halfpenny a week for the first year and one penny afterwards. All the purchases made had to be accounted for and the monthly audit checked by his father.

It was this strict childhood training in the ways of 'business' which fired Wilson's ambition to become a business man himself as soon as his school-days were over. His aim was clear; he determined to have accumulated the sum of twenty thousand pounds before his twenty-fifth birthday, thus making himself a fortune. With his business career in mind, Wilson left school at the age of fifteen and went to work for his grandfather in his wholesale warehouse in Cheapside. His grandfather's ideas of ground his grandson in habits of economy and industry included setting him to work – picking up all the pins he saw lying on the floor of the warehouse and straightening them for further use. Pieces of string also had to be reclaimed and wound up tidily. Naturally, the young Wilson did not appreciate this stage of his training, but he persevered and determined to master the business thoroughly. Realizing that his grandson had inherited the family talent for commercial life, Wilson's grandfather retired when the young man had attained the age of twenty-one, and from then onwards Wilson was free to realize his schoolboy ambition to accumulate a fortune.

It was at this time that Wilson began to run his life with rigid self-discipline. Realizing that he needed physical exercise, and determined to overcome his spinal weakness, he decided to run the five miles from home to his office each day. Determined not to let work-commitments take over his whole life, he devoted time to playing music, and with his first savings bought a fine harmonium which, in later years, he used at mission-meetings. But the mainstream of his young adult life was devoted to the making of money. This singleness of aim, later to be concentrated on working for the destitute, was set on achieving his goal of twenty thousand pounds. Success crowned his speculations, and all his talents of tenacity, imagination and daring were devoted to that end.

Religion had not much part in the young Wilson's life, although he did attend the local non conformist chapel to please his parents, his father being a deacon at Stockwell congregational chapel. However, he had begun to doubt the wisdom of a purely money-making career as this anecdote, told by Wilson in later years, illustrates: 'I was reading in the press of some suppers for burglars, given by one who was himself a reclaimed burglar . . . Though I was making money freely at the time . . . and could easily have afforded a handsome cheque, I gave a paltry 5 shillings to the reclaimed burglar for his good work. He replied saying how delightful it was to be able to help others. It was a discovery to me to find that I could be of use to others with only my money, and although I am ashamed of the miserable sum I sent, my eyes were opened to a new usefulness in life.'

Aged twenty-five, Wilson had more than attained his object; he had accumulated a personal fortune of not twenty, but thirty thousand pounds. But a year later came the day of disaster in business circles known as 'Black Friday'. A series of bank suspensions in London and New York caught many businesses in a vortex of disaster, and one of the hardest hit was Wilson's. Out of the thirty thousand pounds, suddenly only one and a half thousand remained. All that he had given his time, energy and ambition to was lost, shattered, and Wilson had to face failure on a grand scale.

Wilson's first reaction was to become ill. His spinal disorder returned, and for some weeks he was compelled to lie in bed and rest. 'God threw me on my back that I might look up the better', he said later. It was during this time that an aunt, who was a devout member of the Plymouth Brethren, sought to console the embittered young man by telling him of his condition as a sinner and his need for a saviour. At first the aunt's visit infuriated Wilson, but one day she left behind a book called *Grace and Truth* by Mackay for him to read, with the parting exhortation, 'If ever you are worried about your soul read that.' Wilson began with scepticism to read the book that was to change his life. He turned to the chapter which asked, 'Do you feel your sins forgiven?' This seemed to him to be a rather absurd question, since he tended to regard himself not as a 'sinner' but rather as a person with 'faults'. Gradually, as he read the chapter, he realized that he was indeed a sinner, in the fullest sense of the word. He began to understand something of the meaning of Calvary; as he said later, 'At the beginning of the chapter I was a rank outsider. Before I got to the end, I had thrown myself at the feet of Christ and cried, "My Lord, and My God".'

Although Wilson continued to work in the business for a further five years as his father's partner, his ambition and energy were now channelled into mission-work. At first, both he and his wife found satisfaction in helping the Plymouth Brethren in their mission at Blackfriars, and each would attempt to teach the rudiments of bible-study to children of that poor area. Soon they realized the need for something more practical for the prostitutes who frequented Blackfriars, and Wilson used his business skills to raise funds for buying a house near the mission hall and converting it into a rescue home.

The Wilson Carliles did not remain long as Plymouth Brethren, however. Wilson's father had now become a member of the anglican church and Wilson and his wife attended holy communion at the Holy Trinity Church, Richmond, with them on several occasions. This came to the attention of the Brethren at Blackfriars, who sadly denounced Wilson as a 'disorderly brother' and forbade him to break bread with them again. Although they continued to help with some of the social and evangelistic work at Blackfriars, the Carliles drifted gradually away and were eventually confirmed at Clapham parish church.

Evangelistic work continued to occupy much of Wilson's spare time, first in the organization of a Sunday School for poor children in the parish of Holy Trinity, and later becoming involved with the American Evangelists Moody and Sankey's campaign. In 1875, after two years spent in the provinces, Moody and Sankey reached London and opened their campaign in the Agricultural Hall. Hearing that volunteers were needed for the choir, Wilson eagerly offered to join and soon found himself either deputizing for Sankey on the harmonium, or leading the singing of the vast crowds which gathered to hear the famous evangelists.

Another famous evangelist of the time, Professor Henry Drummond, gave Wilson his first taste of preaching. Suddenly leaving the meeting at which he was to speak, Drummond left Wilson alone at the harmonium with the realization that he was in sole charge of the crowd. Somehow, although extremely nervous, Wilson managed to think of some words to say, and realized that laymen could take their share in the work of preaching. Largely because of this experience, in 1877 Wilson offered his service to the Evangelization Society in order to gain some training and experience in preaching. Although not instantly successful as a preacher, one of his efforts being described as 'All stories and anecdotes. No chance for anyone to be converted', he persevered and was soon ready to take the next decisive step in his career. He decided to leave the world of business and enter St John's College, Highbury, to train for ordination.

In those days it was unusual for a married man to enter a theological college and Wilson had to face the prospect of having to support his wife and family during his student days, as well as a long train journey daily from his home at Richmond to Highbury. Besides this, he knew that, in leaving the family business, he was leaving his father without a partner. Determined on his course of action Wilson settled down to study, though he found this the most difficult hurdle of all, feeling all the time that he should be out preaching and meeting human need. However, because of this self-made urgency, he managed to complete the course in less than two years and was ordained to the curacy of St Mary Abbots, Kensington, in 1880.

St Mary's proved to be an ideal place for Wilson. Firstly, he became a member of a large team consisting of the vicar and ten curates representing all parties within the Church. He therefore learned something of the comprehensiveness of the Church of England and its tolerance of varying opinions. Secondly, the parish itself was large and varied: an enormous barracks, a workhouse and a large police station all needed a share of the ministry, as well as the regular congregation. But Wilson felt a special concern, as always, for the poorer people who thronged the streets of Kensington but rarely worshipped in church. With these people in mind he began to show magic-lantern slides in a school hall; the slides attracted crowds of people from the streets and, after the rowdier elements in the crowd had exhausted themselves by cheering and stamping their feet at the comic pictures, Wilson would introduce family prayers as a conclusion to the evening.

But Wilson longed to make still further efforts to reach those who would not reach him, and decided to embark on a venture which led, eventually, to the birth of the Church Army. He began to hold open-air meetings in Kensington High Street at nine in the evening when many people, including coachmen, grooms and servants from the large Kensington houses, were strolling about. Here by a drinking fountain Wilson would speak, at first on his own and later helped by a growing band of volunteers, including a young butler from one house and a groom from another. Soon the little band of workers became known as the 'Church Militant Mission', although various members of the street population termed them 'Carlile's Monkeys'.

As the popularity of Carlile meetings grew, Wilson organized a regular Sunday evening march through the streets to Vestry Hall, then the magistrates' buildings. The procession would carry a banner bearing on it a large cross, and would march singing 'Onward Christian Soldiers' and inviting passers-by to fall-in and join them. At the hall, crowds filled the small room and overflowed into the street; in a window a board would be placed bearing the words, 'full, come earlier next Sunday'. The format of the meeting was described by Wilson thus: 'The hymns and choruses . . . always very bright, the extempore prayers rarely exceeded one minute. The addresses, which generally commenced or ended with some pointed passage, scarcely ever lasted more than three or four minutes . . . [and] . . . were almost invariably from the lips of tradesmen and working people. At the close I went to the magistrates long table in the middle of the hall, and asked all who were desirous of serving Christ, to come and kneel with me and pray for mercy and strength.'

The presence of Wilson's Church Militant Mission in Kensington became impossible to ignore and, besides attracting converts, it also became the focus of attack from a notorious band of young men known as the 'Skeleton Army', who set themselves the task of breaking up all outdoor religious meetings. Many of them wore a scarf-pin or badge with a tiny model of a human skeleton, and a black flag with skull and crossbones often waved over them as they rushed upon a service, delivering a volley of eggs, sticks and stones.

Eventually, both crowds and disturbances grew so great that the Vicar of St Mary Abbots decided, in June 1882, to forbid Wilson to hold further meetings. However, realizing the importance of his curate's work, he encouraged him to found the Church Army as a society. As Wilson and others saw it, the unique quality of the Church Militant Mission lay in the fact that, as Wilson said, '. . . timid exhortation and humble testimonies of working people attracted quite as much attention as did my own preaching' . . . in fact they seemed to produce an even deeper effect on their own class. 'Therefore,' he concluded, 'I ought to . . . try to train working men as Church evangelists and to band them together . . . to assist in Church evangelization.'

So the Church Army was founded in 1882 and Wilson began, together with other founder members, including his sister Marie, to recruit new members. Advertisements were placed in church papers which called for 'Young men . . . full of fire and hard work, ready to give up all for the Lord Jesus.' Applicants must have been surprised by some of the questions included on the form which they were required to fill in: 'Can you use the same homely language in speaking for Christ as for your trade?' 'How much indoor and outdoor persecution can you stand without being angry?' 'Have you ever kept an open-air meeting going for an hour without one person to help you?' Yet these questions underline the difficult and often unpopular work which all members of the Church Army undertook. Frequently attacked by unruly groups such as the Skeleton Army they continued to be mocked mercilessly and pelted with stones, eggs and red ochre powder, which was a favourite missile because of its vivid and long-lasting effect. The word 'army' took on special significance; a literal warfare against sin as the Church Army Corps marched through the often jeering crowds.

Wilson's idea of a military-style army arose, firstly, from the simple need to attract peoples' attentions; hence the banners, bands, processions and uniform–red cord in the buttonhole. But more than this, the Army stood for work outside the church. As an early poster said, 'Instead of inviting people to come to the Church the Army is really the Church going to the people. A Gospel Army without a Church is an imperfect organization, and a Church without an Army is an agency incompetent to reach the masses.'

The concept of the Church Army as part of the Anglican Church was central. Soldiers of the army had to be church-communicants, and adult converts were linked to the church through confirmation. No Church Army work was started without the approval of the Diocesan Bishop concerned, and the activities of all captains and their corps of soldiers were under the control of the local incumbant. When, in 1887, women were invited to train as mission nurses 'for the conversion of souls and ministering to the sick and afflicted' under the leadership of Marie Carlile, the Church realized the unique role which the mission nurses were able to play in parish life. As a contemporary commentator wrote: 'She, (a Church Army mission nurse) . . . can speak to women, sympathize with them and win their confidence far more successfully than anyone who is above them in education and position both social and offical.'

Carlile maintained his own position within the Anglican Church as an ordained minister and was given the living of St Mary-at-Hill in the City of

London, near the Billingsgate fish market, and in 1906 he was given the title of Prebendary Carlile and a stall in St Pauls Cathedral. It was not till 1926 that he devoted himself entirely to Church Army work, by which time every conceivable avenue of service to society was being explored by the continually increasing numbers of Church Army officers. As needs arose within society, so the Army attempted to meet them, always preserving the general pattern of the two branches – evangelistic work and social work. As one officer wrote, 'It is natural that changes should constantly be taking place, especially in the social side of our work where human problems are constantly changing with the changing social pattern.' It is difficult to categorize briefly the changes which arose during Carlile's long life. Prison evangelism was begun as early as 1896; emigration was arranged for men who were considered suitable to go and farm in Canada; new hostels and rehabilitation units were built in poor areas; youth centres, holiday homes and clubs were set up. During the First World War the Church Army established a hospital and many centres in the battle areas, as well as providing ambulances and mobile canteens. Between wars the biggest lasting contribution which the Church Army made was to help with unemployment by assisting a thousand persons a year to emigrate to the colonies.

It is impossible not to tell the story of Wilson Carlile without at the same time telling the story of the Church Army, for the Church Army was the idea he lived for; it represents his life. At the age of ninety, Wilson was still determined to carry both his evangelistic message and his practical help to the 'Joey Billys' of the world. At his birthday party he made a brief speech: 'This is a day of rejoicing for you, but it is a day of humiliation for me. I have been supported by the Archbishop and all the Bishops and by many leading men and women. I have been given money for my work. And yet today there are still criminals in this country, still people sleeping out, still people who never say a prayer.'

It was what had not been done and what still so badly needed doing which always concerned him most. The advent of the Second World War meant new and different opportunities as well as disorganization. In 1942 Wilson, now aged ninety-five, decided it was time to resign and appointed his own successor, the Reverend Hubert Treacher. Three days after the new appointment, on 26 September 1942, Wilson died suddenly. His funeral was held by the Archbishop of Canterbury in St Paul's Cathedral and he was buried in the crypt. The Church Army observes his birthday, January 14, as Founder's Day, with a service in the crypt of St Paul's, but every day Wilson Carlile's spirit is perpetuated by Church Army evangelists who continue to carry on the work begun in 1882.

DONALD SOPER

(1903–)

'It is not in my judgement possible to be a practising Christian today without having a clear idea as to how Christianity is politically interpreted', stated Donald Soper in the BBC programme 'Frankly Speaking' (29 July 1965). Throughout his long life Soper has remained consistent to this belief and has made his position clear, often in the face of opposition and criticism, on the political issues on which he feels strongly. His life-long commitment to pacifism is undoubtedly a central part of his life, as are his strongly-held socialist political views, and both stem from his firm, all-encompassing christian belief. As he says, 'I hold to the words that "all things work together for good to them that love God" and I try to keep my eyes fixed on what I have to do and be, by the grace of God.'

Donald Soper's qualities of commitment and consistency may be traced to his parents who were both persons of impregnable convictions. Both his father and mother shared an ardent christian faith expressed through Wesleyan Methodism. One of the components of their religious conviction was an abhorrence of alcohol so absolute that teetotalism became elevated to the level of a sacred cause. This belief may serve to illustrate Donald's father's strict adherence to principle: he even travelled around lecturing on the evils of drink, equipped with a collection of dummy bottles labelled with the names of various alcoholic liquids which were to be condemned. Donald was later to demonstrate his father's undeviating enthusiasm for a cause in which he believed.

Donald was brought up with his brothers and sisters to believe that he was ultimately accountable to God for the use made of his time and talents. Duties, obligations and, above all, striving to the utmost of one's ability at work and at play, was the pattern of family life. However difficult, and at times exhausting, living by rigid principles may have been, it was certainly happy. The Sopers' home in London was always busy; both parents working – Ernest as a businessman in the City of London and Caroline as a schoolteacher – the children able and eager to strive to give of their best. Their lives were not always spent in earnest endeavour; they had their relaxed moments, whether at home playing musical instruments or going to dances with friends. The family life centered around and was absorbed in the community of the local methodist body: the lively church provided a whole complex of activities both secular and sacred, which provided all the stimulation necessary for the Soper family. They needed and knew no other life. It is not difficult to understand how, at the age of thirteen, Donald's ambition was to become a methodist minister. However, his reaffirmation of this desire came, on a far deeper level, several years later at Cambridge.

It was at Cambridge, where Donald had gone as a student to St Catherine's College in 1921, that his religious and political life was first shaken and then radically altered. For the first time in his life he was away from the influences of home. He read Lecky's *History of Rationalism* and 'at the end of it I was a confessed and complete atheist'. This extreme position did not last long, however, but Donald's faith, to which he returned was never so dogmatic, comprehensive or self-evident as before. As he says, 'I am a Christian agnostic in many things today, and I've learned that the idea of Christianity as something which provides the answers to any question which can conceivably be asked is sheer nonsense.' At Wesley House Donald read philosophy of religion for Part II of his Tripos and began studying to enter the ministry.

Gaining a First at Cambridge, he embarked on his career as a probationer minister at the South London Mission in September 1926 and there became educated in what he had lacked so far – an awareness of other peoples' lives. 'I had lived a sheltered life . . . and Cambridge was not a particularly expansive kind of education in terms of social conditions. I was academically aware of what words like "poverty" and "deprivation" and "poor housing" meant, but to see these things was a profound shock'. His home had taught him the fundamentals of christian living; Cambridge had taught him to think about and sometimes to criticize them; his time at the South London Mission and later, at the Central London Mission, provided him with an insight into the lives of other people who were in those days referred to as 'working class'. Witnessing the poverty of South London, the slums, the unemployment, the misery of the majority of the population, had a deep effect on Donald Soper. He saw for the first time the effects of social injustice and was profoundly affected. In this, of course, he was not alone. As is well known, the 1920s and 1930s were times of political awakening for many, and the majority moved leftward, spurred on by the rise of fascism abroad. Political awakening became radicalization, and for Donald Soper, socialism became, like pacifism, an essential element in his christianity.

That other essential element, pacifism, seems to have emerged even earlier than his early days of ministry during his time at Cambridge, although at that time his feelings were nothing more specific than a general abhorrence of war. It was later that this attitude crystallized into a firm commitment. In 1935 the Reverend Henry Carter, a prominent methodist minister, published an article in the *Methodist Recorder* which announced his conversion to pacifism. Many ministers, including Donald, responded and formed the Methodist Peace Fellowship.

Both these elements - socialism and pacifism - must be seen as an essential framework to Donald Soper's life as a minister and as a human being. He does not hold each ideological belief in a separate vacuum but relates them to the contemporary scene, extending christian pacifism not only to a belief in the inconsistency of Christianity and war but to the whole concept of christian discipleship; extending socialism not only to overtly political action but to a caring attitude towards the individual.

Within this framework of deep conviction and principle, Donald Soper's ministry flowered. In 1929, having completed his three years probation, he was ordained and sent to the Central London Mission to be the first minister of Islington Central Hall. Here, in the vast hall, Donald attracted large congregations by his eloquence, his fervour and his presence. He soon became known as an excellent public speaker. Before long he was broadcasting regularly, building up a broadcasting ministry as well as becoming widely known as an open air speaker at both Tower Hill and Highbury Corner. He soon became 'a new voice of power and influence in the religious life of the metropolis', as one paper described him. His awareness of social need, reinforced by first-hand knowledge of the depression – from his deep involvement in the community centre for the unemployed of Islington – reaffirmed his vigorous and vociferous pacifism and socialism. Not only was he a promising minister but also a prominent political speaker.

In spite of his controversial character, he was appointed in 1936 as superintendent of the West London Mission. At Kingsway, one of the principal Free Church preaching stations in London, Donald was given the chance to expand and use his gifts to full advantage, always acting from the premise that

Christianity is not only a revolutionary doctrine; it is the answer to the needs of the world. The West London Mission became, under his leadership, a great centre for social work: a hostel was erected for ex-prisoners, as well as a girls' hostel and a boys' club: Donald encouraged prison-visiting at Pentonville and inspired young men and women to preach with him at open-air missions. As well as this he continued to broadcast, while his services at Kingsway usually attracted capacity congregations of two thousand.

At the beginning of the war, Donald was blacklisted by the BBC because of his pacifism. This move may be seen as symbolic of his inevitably somewhat ostracized position during the dark years of the war. He did not, however, as some other pre-war pacifists, compromise in any way but continued to preach pacifism at Tower Hill and on Hyde Park Corner. He did not suffer, as did many of his Peace-Pledge-Union contemporaries, from any moral dilemma. When asked how it was possible to live with pacifism on the one hand and the knowledge of Hitler's concentration camps on the other he replied, '. . . to me the answer to this terrible violence never appeared to be the necessity for more violence.' Throughout the war he bore witness to his statement that 'absolute pacifists should in peace strive against war and in war devote themselves to the service of the people.' His all-encompassing ministry at Kingsway continued: as one observer reported in 1940, 'At Kingsway Hall there was not a vacant seat. Dr Donald Soper said that . . . the spiritual potency and power which could be generated and used at such services . . . were equal to the task of establishing and maintaining on earth peace and truth and all those lovely things which now seemed so remote.'

The war ended and Donald's pacifism was carried forward into the nuclear age. Controversial as ever, he spoke at the 1950 methodist conference at Bradford, saying that, in effect, if it came to a choice of taking part in a Third World War or allowing Britain to be overrun by communist forces, he would choose the latter. This statement antagonized not only many of the conference delegates but also many of the general public. A letter to the *Daily Mail* complained: 'Switching on to the Home Service, just prior to the 6pm news on 9 August we were horrified to hear that Children's Hour Prayers are to be led by the Reverend Donald Soper. In view of this gentleman's recently expressed conviction that Communism in Britain is preferable to another war, surely the BBC, as a publicly subsidized body, should immediately terminate any contracts which he may have with them.' Undeterred by his unpopularity in some quarters, Donald maintained that 'those who take the sword perish by the sword . . . we do not know what happens to those who take the sword of the spirit because we have not tried it out on a large scale.'

A founder member of the Campaign for Nuclear Disarmament in 1957, Donald marched several times to Aldermaston and became a familiar figure at the head of demonstrations; 'The march was the beginning and not the end of the intention', he has said. The end of the intention was, of course, to persuade the Government to unilaterally reject the Bomb, the manufacture and use of it. And to this intention Donald Soper remains committed. As a colleague in the Methodist Peace Fellowship, the Reverend David Francis, wrote; 'he remains patiently and patently consistent. You may not agree with him, but you always know where he stands.'

Donald retired from the superintendency of the West London Mission in 1978, but did not retire from public life. He still maintains an active presence in debates both political and otherwise, but instead of debating on Tower Hill or Hyde Park Corner as he used to, he now uses his wide knowledge of human concerns and his gift for public speaking on radio or television, where he is often to be seen discussing some area of current affairs. His political and religious beliefs remain relatively unchanged but never stale and are, perhaps, best expressed by the prayer he prayed at a service in the crypt chapel of the House of Commons for members of Harold Wilson's Government in 1964. The text of the prayer tells of the unchanging vision of the man: 'Oh God, grant us a vision of our land, fair as it might be, A land of righteousness where none might wrong his neighbour, A land of plenty where evil and poverty shall be done away; A land of brotherhood where all success shall be founded on service, and honour shall be given on excellence alone; A land of peace, where order shall not rest on force, but on the love of all for the common life and weal; Bless our efforts to make the vision a living reality; Inspire and strengthen each one of us that we may give time, thought and sacrifice to speed the day of its coming.'

GROUP CAPTAIN LEONARD CHESHIRE

(1917-   )

As he lay ill with tuberculosis, Cheshire kept his eyes fixed on the picture which hung at the foot of his bed. It was a life-sized reproduction of the Holy Shroud of Turin. 'There, for a full month,' he said, 'I did little but lie and look at that Holy Face . . . Before such a face as this, so ill-used, yet so serene, so majestic yet so gentle, who could fail to be moved? Who could fail to see its reflection in the poor, the maimed, the sick, the dying, the unwanted, the lonely, in all those who suffer or are in need from whatever cause? And who, having seen all this, could be content to lie back and rest so long as anywhere in the world there remains but one human being in want or distress?' The story of Group Captain Cheshire centres around this image; the image of a deeply compassionate man whose efforts to help those in need have been labelled by some as wildly optimistic and by others as inconsistent, but who nevertheless succeeded in originating an impressively flourishing scheme – the Leonard Cheshire Foundation.

Leonard Cheshire began life in Chester, the son of an eminent lawyer. He attended Stowe school where he is remembered by the headmaster's secretary as being 'small, slim and quiet' and a lover of tennis. He worked hard and seemed destined as he left school for Merton College, Oxford, to become another academic lawyer in an academic family. But, as he says, 'It was at Oxford that I started NOT to work.' Certainly it was whilst a student that Cheshire seemed to discover within himself a love of taking risks. At this time in his young life the risks were irresponsible and silly; driving a fast car; disappearing to London all night; drinking too much. It seemed as if he was experimenting with fear, testing himself to see how far he could stretch his foolhardiness; a preliminary skirmish with what was soon to be the real thing.

After achieving a Second Class degree, Cheshire immediately joined the RAF. The Second World War had not yet begun but, having learnt to fly in the university air squadron, Cheshire was granted a commission in the air force, so satisfying his ever-present need for excitement. Very soon after this, war was declared and Cheshire, along with many other young people of the thirties decade, felt that 'the war gave me a motive for life and an authority to live under. I was glad to get into it.'

He was posted to the 102 Squadron of Whitley Bombers, and here began his brilliant career, becoming one of the youngest group captains at the early age of twenty-four, and receiving many awards as the war progressed. Of all his many acts of courage during the war, probably the part he played in destroying Hitler's fortified secret weapon installations at Wizernes and Watten is the most well known. Barnes Wallis invented the bomb which was to drop beside these concrete rocket houses; Cheshire trained and led the 617 Squadron whose task it was to lay the bomb alongside the target. 'We alone', Cheshire relates, 'now possessed the equipment and the bomb capable of destroying the five monstrous launching-platforms that the Germans were building in the Pas-de-Calais.'

After flying one hundred missions Cheshire was ordered by the Air Vice Marshall to retire in order to rest. To mark his achievements of leadership and courage, King George VI invested him with a third DSO and the Victoria Cross. Cheshire speaks of his VC thus: '. . . my VC was given to me, not for anything I did, but for all of 617 Squadron'. It was while he was enjoying a rest from the war and sitting in a London night-club, that he took part in a discussion which was to have a long-lasting effect on him. Someone was talking about God and what God was and Cheshire interrupted: 'Well, I know perfectly well what God is. God is an inner conscience that we all have; it tells us what to do in the circumstances that we are in.' 'Absolute nonsense', retorted a woman-friend. 'God is a Person, and you know it perfectly well.' For some reason the conversation took root in Cheshire's mind and, in the months ahead, he was to reflect upon it. He realized that if a personal God exists, as Christianity maintains, then there must be certain implications for oneself.

However, he had to put this contemplation to the back of his mind, as he was summoned to end his period of rest and fly to the Mariana Islands in the

Pacific to work with the American Air Force on what was to be the final act of the war. His one hundred and first mission was about to begin; he and Sir William Penney, the atomic scientist, were to be the official observers when the second atomic bomb was dropped on Nagasaki in Japan.

As Cheshire looked down from his seat in the American aeroplane, flying in brilliant sunshine at thirty-nine thousand feet, he saw, far below, the writhings of the dying city of Nagasaki. The blinding flash in the sky followed by the ball of fire above, giving out a belching haze of white smoke, darkened the summer day. There was a sense of wind and heat. Later Cheshire was to learn that the atom bomb had killed forty thousand and left sixty thousand of the total population completely homeless. By comparison, in the whole of the war only thirty thousand Londoners had been killed by air-attack. The appalling spectacle imprinted itself forever on Cheshire's mind. Although he had taken part in so many bombing attacks himself, he had never before felt the need to face the conflict of killing and christian ethics. Now, confronted with a horrifying example of man's destructiveness to man, he felt revolted and dismayed. More than that, he felt that 'to conceive that all this can happen, means changing your fundamental concept of what is possible and what is not possible. . .' Although never a pacifist, Cheshire had this to say about nuclear weapons in 1945, words which now have a prophetic ring: 'Today it [the bomb] carries the power of victory, because, so far as we know, no-one else possesses it. Tomorrow, when the whole world possesses it . . . it will merely carry the power of destruction over an unprotected enemy which will be immeasurably greater than anything we have previously known.'

The war ended. The attraction of communal life, which Cheshire had become used to during the war-years, linked with his enthusiastic concern for bettering the standard of living for as many people as possible, led him to form a community for ex-servicemen and women called VIP, which stood for 'Vade in Pacem' or 'Go in Peace', and bought Gumley Hall, near Market Harborough in Leicestershire, which the community took over in 1946. He then bought a house in Hampshire called Le Court and the community expanded to fill this as well.

But VIP was short-lived. Cheshire, worn out by the war, took a holiday in Canada and rested in British Columbia for six months, dwelling on the unanswered questions posed during that night in the London club. It was while he was enjoying this contemplative life that he received a telegram, 'VIP in trouble. Return immediately'. The community had built up enormous debts and had to be disbanded, Cheshire selling Gumley Hall and retaining Le Court as a house now divided into self-service flats.

Then Cheshire's life took a new and unexpected change of direction; this time towards a more permanent goal. One of the former members of VIP,

Arthur Dykes, had developed inoperable cancer and was in hospital near Le Court. Unable to do more, the hospital wanted to discharge him, but he had nowhere to go. Cheshire took a risk which this time was to have long-lasting consequences; he offered to take Arthur back to Le Court and nurse him, himself. Thus it could be claimed that Arthur Dykes was the first Cheshire Home resident, although Le Court did not become known as a Cheshire Home until after Arthur Dykes' death.

Dykes and Cheshire came to know each other well during the months before Arthur Dykes died. A roman catholic, he often talked of the religion which meant so much to him, and Cheshire, still seeking to identify his personal God and how God speaks most authoritatively to the world today, was very interested in discussing religious issues. He was also helped by a book of Arthur Dykes', *One Lord, One Faith*, written by Vernon Johnson, an ex-anglican priest. At last, as Cheshire said, 'The groping after truth had ceased; the doubts and waverings of the past were gone; in their place, a calm, invincible certainty. I knew I must go to Father Clarks [the local priest] and ask him for instruction into the Roman Catholic Church.' On 23 December 1948, Cheshire was received into the Roman Catholic Church.

Meanwhile, Arthur Dykes had died peacefully, but not before proposing to Cheshire that others in a similar plight to himself should be given the chance to come and live at le Court. Cheshire, Dykes maintained, had a God-given vocation to care for suffering people. Cheshire was not convinced of this at first, but other patients began to arrive; an old aunt of Cheshire's and then a man with tuberculosis who had been referred by a London chest clinic. The way was now clear; against the advice of many friends Cheshire decided to put his confidence in God and obey providence. If people continued to come, he would continue to look after them. By the spring of 1949 staff had been appointed, residents were pouring in, and Cheshire had to start a waiting-list. He took in people of all ages and with a variety of complaints, the only criteria for admission being that they were genuinely in need, and believed Le Court to be the best place for them. Providence was also relied on for matters of finance; the disabled residents paid what they could; voluntary donations and local hospital schemes made up the balance.

But the constant strain of caring for the sick and managing Le Court, even with the help of a trained social worker, Francis Jeram, and the support of his parents who had retired nearby, proved too much and Cheshire became ill. By 1951, after a period of rest, he was advised to take a job away from Le Court and lead a less tiring life. This meant that he would no longer manage Le Court, and so a board of trustees was appointed. Francis Jeram was given the post of warden, and Cheshire sadly relinquished his control but consented to his name being used as a means of attracting funds. Thus the first 'Cheshire Home' came into being.

Cheshire accepted a post at Vickers Armstrong where he was to be involved in munitions research with, by coincidence, Barnes Wallis. Since Cheshire believed that a Third World War was inevitable, and that it was the Government's duty to prepare the defences of Britain, he did not feel that he was violating the convictions which he had formed since the bombing of Nagasaki. He was posted to Cornwall, as a research expert, to a testing-site on a disused airfield at Predannack.

It was here in Cornwall that stage two of the development of the Cheshire Homes came into being. An ex-naval frogman who had developed severe epilepsy wrote to Cheshire saying that he needed a permanent residence. Cheshire immediately offered him the use of his own house at Predannack. Noticing the many disused, dilapidated buildings in the area of the airfield, Cheshire determined to start a second home. In January 1951 he found a structurally-sound Nissan hut, obtained a monthly tenancy from the Air Ministry and began, with local help, to rebuilt it. The new home, St Teresa's, was opened in May 1951, built from funds raised entirely by the people of Cornwall.

Soon after the opening of St Teresa's it was decided to form the Cheshire Trust to own both Homes. The Trust began to attract money from ever wider sources, including sixty-five thousand pounds from the Carnegie Foundation for the building of a new home in the grounds of Le Court to replace the old house, which was literally sinking in its foundations, eaten away by a previously unnoticed underground stream.

By this time it had become clear to Cheshire that his job with Vickers was an empty distraction and not at all part of his main task which he now knew with certainty to be the organization of homes for the sick and handicapped. He left Vickers in 1952 with no regrets, and concentrated on opening a third home near St Teresa's, called Holy Cross, for patients with mental disabilities.

At about this time Cheshire, who had suffered bouts of what was thought to be flu throughout 1951, was given a chest X-ray. This revealed that his left lung had an ominous cavity: he had tuberculosis, probably caught from one of the patients whom he had been looking after. Faced with this grave news, a friend remarked that 'he just gave a typical grin and nearly laughed out loud'.

He was transferred to the King Edward VII sanatorium, Midhurst, Sussex, where he was to stay from August 1952 until the winter of 1954. During this time he had four severe operations and was, for part of the time, severely ill. Yet he used his time constructively, seeing, perhaps for the first time, the role that his homes played in the modern world. It seemed that they filled a gap in the structure of the health service and that they would continue to proliferate to fulfil this unmet need. Cheshire also realized that his personal presence would not be enough; moreover, it would no longer be necessary as the Trust would administer the building and maintenance of new homes.

Thirdly, Cheshire was advised during this period of physical inactivity and mental reorganization, to keep the Trust non-denominational. Since he had originally appealed to people of all religions and had received a magnificent response, the awakening desire to help the sick and handicapped was, obviously, a non-denominational one and must remain so.

Today the homes continue to proliferate and, at present in 1986, there are seventy-four Cheshire Homes in the United Kingdom, while the Trust is affiliated with a further 147 in forty-seven countries overseas. Currently five thousand physically and/or mentally handicapped people are receiving residential care in Cheshire Homes worldwide and, besides this, the Trust runs a family support service and the most recent innovation is the installation of computer facilities in some homes, thus giving patients an added stimulus and sense of independence.

Leonard Cheshire's life may be seen as a process of risk-taking; a gigantic obstacle-race which must be run because it is there. And of all the risks, the most enduring was his decision, back in 1948, to take in and look after Arthur Dykes, the first patient to receive the Cheshire-Home treatment. The caring environment and attitude which he offered Dykes remain central to the concept of Cheshire Homes today. The aims of a Cheshire home are defined thus: 'A Cheshire Home is a place of shelter physically, and of encouragement spiritually; a place where the residents can acquire a sense of belonging and of ownership by contributing in any way within their capabilities to its functioning and development; a place to share with others, and from which to help others less fortunate; a place in which to gain confidence and develop independence and interests; a place of hopeful endeavour and not of passive disinterest.

CICELY SAUNDERS

(1918–   )

It was a dying Polish Jew called David Tasma who acted as catalyst and inspiration to Cicely's founding of the hospice movement. In 1947 Cicely, a qualified nurse and almoner, was called upon to arrange for David's admission to hospital. Aged only forty, David had inoperable cancer and, by the time he was admitted to hospital, he had been told by Cicely that he had not much longer to live. Although at first they had only a professional relationship, the lonely man, who was without relatives or friends in this country, and the unfulfilled young woman, soon fell deeply in love. They had not long together; only twenty-five meetings in all before David died, but in that time their relationship grew with a rapid intensity. Besides expressing their personal feelings for each other, their meetings took on another dimension as they discussed how the needs of the dying person could best be met.

Cicely had spent all her young adult life with the persistent desire to help other people, first by training to become a nurse and then as a medical social worker. But still she felt she needed to have more, wider opportunities than her training and work seemed to provide. By becoming deeply involved with David she found her answer; she realized the lack of care for the terminally ill. Not only was there a desperate need for more continuous and skilful pain-relief, but there were other considerations also. The patient must be seen as an individual and his individual social, spiritual and emotional needs must be met; only then could the dying patient achieve a coming-to-terms with his disease. David shared her enthusiasm: for his part, he felt that if his early death were to plant the seeds of a new, creative way of helping other dying patients, then his life would not have been as pointless and wasted as he had bitterly felt before. He became determined that Cicely should carry through their joint ideas and left her five hundred pounds in his will, saying, 'I'll be a window in your home'.

At last Cicely knew what she had to do; she had to nourish this idea and allow it to bear fruit. In a sense, her period of waiting was over and from now on her life was motivated in one direction, the care of the dying.

Cicely's life and career up to the time of her friendship with David had been a mixture of unhappiness and disappointment. Sent to Roedean at the age of fourteen, the fashionable girls' boarding school near Brighton, she was wretchedly unhappy. Too shy to make many friends, she felt a lost misfit during her time there. Then, having failed to be accepted by two Oxford colleges, she was finally accepted by the Society for Home Students, later called St Anne's College, Oxford. Here she began to read politics, philosophy and economics but the Second World War intervened and Cicely decided by leave Oxford after her first year and enrol as a nurse. In this case it was the war which pushed Cicely in the right direction: she had wanted to be a nurse since childhood but her parents had dissuaded her; now the war-effort gave added incentive to her inclination.

She was accepted at St Thomas's Hospital in November 1940 and spent the next three years undergoing the demanding training of a 'Nightingale nurse'. The Nightingale Training School was evacuated to various mental hospitals and homes for the mentally subnormal situated in the surburban countryside round London, but the quality of nursing expected of the students was as high as it had always been. For the first time in her life Cicely felt that she belonged to the life she led. She was happy; she made friends and was a natural nurse. As a friend and contemporary well remembers; 'Cicely's ability was striking. Even then she always seemed to have finished every job first . . . she always managed to have done her work and also to be around to help people who hadn't finished in time.' But Cicely suffered from continual back-ache and, towards the end of her training, only survived by spending her off-duty time lying down. Suddenly, during a period of night duty, her back became much worse. She was sent to the hospital orthopaedic surgeon who insisted that she stop nursing immediately. She received the honours certificate, silver medal standard, but never worked as a nurse again.

Cicely was bitterly disappointed; but decided to

train as a medical social worker, known in those days as an almoner: this would, she thought, keep her in close touch with the patients and their needs. For this training she returned to her old college, now known as St Anne's Society, where she confounded her old tutor who had previously thought her abilities 'ordinary second to third class', by gaining distinctions in her final examinations. The next stage of her almoner's training was spent in London, attached to the Institute of Almoners in Tavistock Square and doing practical work in various hospitals. The head social worker, who supervised Cicely's work during this period, perspicaciously observed that 'She needed a much broader canvas. She was someone who had an enormous amount to give in a way which would be revealed.'

At about this time, Cicely spent a holiday in Cornwall with some friends, all evangelical christians. Although not a committed christian herself, Cicely had for years felt the need for a religious faith. It was here with her friends that Cicely felt that God spoke to her. She experienced the conviction that she was under the control of the Lord, that he was in charge of her life, and she returned to London elated and enthusiastic.

She returned to take up her first post as a qualified almoner at St Thomas's Hospital at the Northcote Trust, a specialised branch of the hospital, caring for cancer patients. It was here that she met David. After his death, knowing beyond doubt that she wanted to work with the dying but unsure of what to do about it, Cicely began to work voluntarily in her spare time at St Luke's, a home for the dying near her flat. St Lukes had a powerful influence on Cicely; it had embodied, since its opening in 1893 as 'A Home for the Dying Poor', many of the concepts which she and David had found to be vital in the care of the terminally ill. One of the visiting sisters wrote in 1905, 'Although all the patients are alike in that they are "dying", each has his own separate life, and it is the duty of the visiting sister to regard with absolute sanctity the individuality of each one, and try and reach that which makes the man HIMSELF, and does not belong to another.' To see the concept of the individual put into practice was inspiring for Cicely, as was the St Luke's concept of pain-relief. Analgesics were used so skilfully that the patients remained relatively pain-free and alert up to the moment of their death. Only a nudge was needed to set Cicely going towards her vocation and that nudge was provided by a St Thomas' consultant who advised her to 'Go and read Medicine. It's the doctors who desert the dying'.

Although Cicely was now thirty-three and would have to start her medical training with eighteen-year-olds, and although she had never studied science at school, she was not deterred. In fact her age gave her both a maturity and a single-mindedness of purpose which enabled her to qualify with honours in surgery and win a prize for obstetrics and gynaecology. During her training Cicely never lost sight of her main objective and, as soon as she had qualified, she began research into pain in the terminally ill. She began to visit St Joseph's Hospice in Hackney, observing the patients and evaluating the use of drugs.

At that time St Joseph's contained one hundred and fifty beds, between forty and fifty for patients with terminal malignant disease, the rest for those with long-term illnesses, or those who were frail and elderly and had no homes. Run by nuns, the medical care was kindly but unsophisticated, and there was no resident doctor. Cicely was indeed an innovation. The fundamental change she made was in the administering of drugs, copying the methods used at St Luke's. She also introduced the scrupulous keeping of patients' records and, above all, tried to involve the patients' families in the illness while encouraging more freedom for the patients, including more flexible visiting hours and more choice in how they wanted to spend their time. One aspect of patient care needed no improvement; the emotional care of those at St Joseph's was never less than loving and at no time did a sense of failure pervade the atmosphere as it often did when nursing terminal disease in general hospitals.

During Cicely's time at St Joseph's, she finally crystallized her plans for the formation of her own hospice. To clarify her long-held beliefs about the care of the dying she wrote two papers. The first entitled *The Need*, pointed out that the prerequisites of caring for the terminally ill or badly disabled were love and skill, and these two qualities were not always to be found in equal measure in wards of general hospitals or even, necessarily, in a home environment. Her second paper *The Scheme*, confidently outlined the plans for her own hospice, asserting the central idea of hospice-care as being a combination of meeting spiritual and emotional needs with the very best practical medical attention. Her hospice vision was modelled to a large extent on St Joseph's, especially in her aim that the staff were to be people who had chosen the work, loved it and would establish a sense of security and community for the patients. After much discussion with friends and advisors, the hospice, to be known as St Christopher's, was given charitable status and a board of trustees appointed in 1961. Now the fund-raising had to begin.

It was while working to acquire funds that Cicely fell in love with another Pole, Antoni Michniewicz, who was dying at St Joseph's. Antoni had left Poland as a prisoner during the war, eventually serving in the army in the Middle East: his wife had recently died and he had only one relative, a daughter. Again, Cicely's relationship was short and passionate and again, inevitably, it ended in death. This time Cicely had to mourn, not only for Antoni, but for her beloved father who had died at almost the same time. She fell into a period of prolonged grieving, which may be seen as a preparation to help suffering through suffering herself. It was a long time before Cicely ceased to grieve, but her consolation lay in her knowledge that she was 'a member of the community of suffering', as a book by Dr H.

Moule on bereavement reminded her. 'Your loss, your pain, brings you into a sacred fellowship, a large yet intimate companionship', Dr Moule asserted.

During this unhappy and painful period in Cicely's life she was busy fund-raising and soon her plans for St Christopher's came to the interested attention of several charitable trusts who offered large sums of money. Cicely decided that the hospice building must be purpose-built, near enough to London for the community to feel part of the bustle of city life, and south of the river so that it would not be competing with St Joseph's for funds. Eventually a site was found in Sydenham and, with her vision of the hospice intact and clear, Cicely had only to give it outward form with the help of an architect, Justin Smith.

On 22 March 1965 the building was begun and for the next two years the work proceeded – time filled with excitement as the hospice gradually materialized, and apprenhension as funds had to be raised quickly and in large amounts. However, all went well and the opening ceremony was performed on schedule by Princess Alexandra on 24 July 1967. It had been a long time since David Tasma's death in 1947, with Cicely's resolution to care for the dying. David's gift of five hundred pounds had, indeed, provided a window in the hospice, or, rather, the hospice had been built around his gift of a window.

Now, nearly twenty years after its beginning, St Christopher's has earned its place as the mother of the modern hospice movement. It has grown and changed, but has always kept its ideological base. One of Cicely's main concepts is that the patients should not be thought of impersonally as 'the dying' but should be involved as part of a relaxed, caring community. St Christopher's achieves this sense of communal caring by incorporating the wider community, not only patients' families, but retired members of staff and volunteers, as well as a playgroup for children of the staff. The extended family of St Christopher's provides the patient with the security of a community of which he/she becomes a important part; an essential element in a corporate act of caring. Love and death, always inextricably linked in Cicely's life, have become woven together at St Christopher's. The christian foundation of St Christopher's had evolved with Cicely's own evolving spiritual life. Finding, after the deaths of Antoni and her father, that the evangelical church no longer satisfied her needs, she eventually became a more broadly-based anglican, and she has always been a respecter of all religions. St Christopher's reflects this attitude; the chapel occupies a central position in the building and is essentially ecumenical; there is a full-time anglican chaplain, but the religious climate of the hospice is determined mainly by the staff who are all involved with the spiritual care of the patient, believing that the dying person needs, above all, someone to listen and understand. Profound loneliness of the dying is not treatable by drugs but by understanding, and if loving-understanding is given, religion just happens, believes Cicely. And loving-understanding means being truthful and facing the reality of death with the patient, telling the patient of his condition if the situation demands it, but not thrusting it upon him before he is ready for it.

Above all, then, Cicely Saunders believes that empathy with the patient on the part of staff and relatives is vital if the quality of life is to be as comfortable and meaningful as possible. In this way, dying becomes not evidence of medical failure, but a deeply enriching experience for all involved. Regular giving of pain-killing drugs, as well as alleviation of other symptoms such as nausea, depression and breathlessness by the proper use of medication, all combine to produce a feeling of relaxed trust. Besides this the nurses, by taking time to know the patients so well, are aware of their needs, however small, and, because of the high nurse/patient ratio, are able to give all the time necessary to meet them.

Cicely's life has been a long struggle, with many disappointments, to achieve fulfilment. In middle-age, recognized as the founder of the modern hospice movement, she has been showered with honours, being made a Dame in 1980 and being awarded the Templeton Prize for progress in religion in 1981. The international spread of Cicely's ideas on terminal care is ever growing and she has lectured with great success in America, being made an honorary Doctor of Science by Yale University in 1969. As well as professional fulfilment, Cicely's personal life became transformed when she met Marian Bohusz, a Polish painter, whose paintings fill the hospice. Eventually, after a long and happy friendship, they married in 1980.

Cicely's remarkable life may be seen as one of the most creative undertakings of this century. Using her own pain and loss as catalysts she has, by her hard work, tenacity and vision, transformed them into a creative undertaking to change the face of death for millions of people. Her concern is to make death more tolerable, to allow people to 'live until they die', as she says, and to this end she is now concerned that the rest of the medical profession deal with pain and death by using her techniques. She is particularly concerned that doctors do not abandon patients once they are beyond care, but allow them, as R.L. Fulton writes in *Death and Identity*, 'the dignified death which proclaims the significance of all men'.

MARTIN LUTHER KING JUNIOR

(1929–1968)

'In a world facing the revolt of ragged and hungry masses of God's children; in a world torn between the tensions of East and West, white and coloured, individualists and collectivists; in a world whose cultural and spiritual power lags so far behind her technical capabilities that we live each day on the verge of nuclear annihilation; in this world non-violence is no longer an option for intellectual analysis, it is an imperative for action.' So wrote Martin Luther King in his book *The Trumpet of Conscience*, 1968.

Non-co-operation and non-violent resistance were Martin Luther King's methods of awakening a sense of morality in one's opponents, a basic humanity which, Luther King believed, was present in everyone and would one day become the unifying principle of life. As he said on another occasion: 'At the centre of non-violence stands the principle of love . . . the oppressed people of the world must not succumb to the temptation of becoming bitter . . . to retaliate in kind would do nothing but intensify the existence of hate in the Universe.'

Martin Luther King was born in Atlanta, Georgia, on 15 January 1929, the son of a negro baptist minister. He learned about segregation early in life when his white friends, with whom he used to play, were sent to a school for white people, while he attended the negro elementary school. A clever child, he nevertheless had to attend local segregated schools for coloured people which were inferior academically from their white counterparts. In spite of this, he graduated from Morehouse College in 1948 when he was only nineteen, but even before this he had decided that his vocation lay in becoming ordained for the ministry. He was ordained into the Ebenezer Church and became an assistant pastor, aged eighteen. Martin, being so intellectually able, was determined not to stop his studying at this point, and accepted a place at Crozer Theological Seminary, Pennsylvania, although his father warned him, 'You're mighty young to go to Crozer.' However, Martin's father need not have feared; Martin was more than equal to the challenge and graduated in June 1951, winning the award for most outstanding student as well as a fellowship for graduate study. Determined to complete his studies by achieving a Ph.D., Martin moved to Boston University in the autumn of 1951. It was during this time that he first became preoccupied with an intellectual quest for a method which would eliminate social evil, including the evil of segregation. The problem of racial injustice had become part of Martin's life since his early teenage years, when he first formed his belief that segregation was both rationally inexplicable and morally unjustifiable. He mentions a specific example of his personal feelings in a sermon, *Pilgrimage to Non-Violence*. 'I could never accept my having to sit in the back of a bus or in a segregated section of a train. The first time that I was seated behind a curtain in a dining-car I felt as though a curtain had been dropped on my self-hood.' Part of his reading during his years at Boston led him to study the life and teachings of Mahatma Gandhi: he continues in the same sermon, 'As I read his works I became deeply fascinated by his campaigns of non-violent resistence . . . I came to see for the first time that the Christian doctrine of love, operating through the Gandhian method of non-violence, is one of the most potent weapons available, to an oppressed people in their struggle for freedom.'

Martin was not ready, at this stage, to follow up Gandhi's philosophy with any action of his own. By the time he finished studying for his Ph.D. he had become convinced, however, that he must turn his back on the freer, more cultural life of the North and on further academic work and return to the South to become a pastor. 'I'm going back South. I am going to live in the South because that is where I'm needed', he told his new wife, Coretta.

Coretta, whom Martin had met while she was studying music at Boston Conservatory, was a talented singer and did not want to return to the South, knowing from her own childhood experiences as a negro in Alabama the stifling clamp of segregation. However, Martin was both enthusiastic and determined and so the couple moved to Montgomery, Alabama, where Martin became the pastor of Dexter

Avenue Baptist Church in September 1954. Neither of them, of course, had any idea that they would shortly be involved in a crisis in which Gandhi's principles of non-violence would be applicable.

Yet, after a year of serene and uncomplicated life, during which time the Luther King's first child, Volanda, was born, such a crisis was to erupt. During this year, following up his feeling of deep commitment to work against segregation Luther King became an active member of the National Association of the Advancement of Coloured People as well as a member of the Alabama Council on Human Relations. Thus he naturally assumed a leading position in the Montgomery bus protest, which was to change the direction of his life. In Montgomery the city buses reserved all front seats on their vehicles for white people, while the negroes would have to crowd to the back. On 1 December 1955, Mrs Rosa Parks, a forty-two year old seamstress boarded a bus to go home after a long day working and shopping. The bus was crowded and Mrs Parks found a seat in the back section, only to be ordered by the bus-conductor to give up her seat to a white man. As she said later, 'I was just plain tired, and my feet hurt'. She refused to give her place up, was arrested and taken to the court-house. This was not the first action of its kind, but this time the arrest inflamed the black population. A meeting was held in Dexter Avenue Church by Luther King and fellow ministers, and it was agreed unanimously to boycott the buses. At first Luther King wondered if he were doing the right thing, but he argued that the boycott was to be used 'to give birth to freedom . . . Our concern [is] not to put the bus company out of business, but to put justice in business.' Enthusiasm for the boycott swept through the fifty thousand black population of Montgomery and an organization was quickly formed called the Montgomery Improvement Association, of which Luther King was voted leader. Another mass meeting was held, this time so crowded that five thousand had to stand outside the church listening to speeches and songs relayed by loud speakers. Luther King first spoke of the feelings of black people, 'We are here this evening to say to those who have mistreated us for so long, that we are tired. Tired of being segregated and humiliated'. He went on to state his philosophy of non-violence. 'No-one must be intimidated to keep them from riding the buses. Our method must be persuasion, not coercion . . . Once again we must hear the words of Jesus. "Love your enemies. Bless them that curse you. Pray for them that despitefully use you".'

It was decided that the boycott would continue until the following demands should be guaranteed: courteous treatment by bus operators; passengers to be seated on a first come, first served basis – negroes sitting from the back forwards, Whites from front to back – and that negro drivers were to be employed on predominantly negro routes. The boycott lasted over a year, during which time Luther King's life and the lives of his wife and daughter were in constant danger. They suffered from repeated threatening phone calls, one of which Luther King recalled in his sermon *Our God is Able*; 'I was about to doze off when the telephone rang. An angry voice said, "Listen, nigger, we've taken all we want from you. Before next week you'll be sorry you ever came to Montgomery".' Not long after this their house was bombed, but fortunately the family escaped unharmed. Besides this, Luther King was goaled twice. But these attempts at intimidation only succeeded in raising the enthusiasm of Luther King's followers and he soon became a national figure. It was during his trial for organizing the boycott, one year after its inception, on 13 November 1956, that Luther King was handed a slip of paper. It stated that 'The United States Supreme Court today affirmed a decision declaring Alabama's state and local laws requiring segregation on buses unconstitutional'. The boycott was over.

But the problems raised by the bus boycott did not disappear with the passing of this law. Fury and frustration built up amongst extremist white racists; some nights the Ku Klux Klan would drive through the streets of the negro section of town, dressed in their white robes and pointed hoods; buses were stoned and shots were even fired into them; one night three negro churches and the homes of two leading negroes were bombed. In spite of this reaction, the boycott was lifted and the buses desegregated. In January 1957 sixty black ministers assembled in Atlanta to form the Southern Christian

Leadership Conference (SCLC), and to continue the civil rights movement. Luther King was elected president. The SCLC's strategy was to use non-violence as a powerful and effective method of confrontation, as it had been in the bus boycott. As Luther King said in his sermon, *Loving Your Enemies*, 'To our most bitter opponents we say, "We shall match your capacity to inflict suffering by our capacity to endure suffering . . . do to us what you will and we shall continue to love you . . . We shall so appeal to your hearts and conscience that we shall win YOU in the process and our victory will be a double victory".'

Counteracting hatred with love was to prove an increasingly difficult ideal for Luther King to maintain amongst the black population, who were becoming ever more restive under continuing racial discrimination. On the anniversary of Lincoln's birthday, 12 February 1958, twenty-one mass meetings were held in key southern cities. Luther King spoke these words at one of them; 'Let us make our intentions clear. We must and shall be free. We want freedom – NOW. We do not want freedom fed to us in teaspoons over another one hundred and fifty years.' However, progress was slow: Luther King requested President Eisenhower to push for a new civil rights bill, but the President would not be committed. It became apparent to Luther King that, if his leadership of the SCLC was to act as a catalyst for breakdown of segregation, he must leave Montgomery and move to Atlanta where the headquarters of SCLC was situated and that he must take on a less taxing pastoral role. He and his family moved to Atlanta in 1960 where he became assistant pastor at his father's church.

Shortly after this move, in February 1960, the 'sit-in' campaigns began. A negro student at college in North Carolina was refused service at the bus terminal lunch-counter. Hearing of this, other black and white students, as well as non-student sympathizers, sat in segregated eating places, quietly but insistently demanding service. The 'sit-ins' spread to South Carolina, Tennesee and Virginia; non-violence, which was to become the anthem of the Freedom Movement, was first sung. Based on a negro church hymn, 'We Shall Overcome', with its message of courage and resolve, it was sung at one rally after another until no meeting could end without it. The 'sit-ins' successfully ended segregation at lunch-counters in many southern cities, but not all, and the SCLC turned its attention to one of Atlanta's most important department stores. When Martin Luther King and seventy-five students entered the store and demanded lunch service, Luther King and some of the students were arrested. Later, charges against the students were dropped, but Luther King was charged with violating his probation on an extremely minor traffic offence. To the amazement and horror of all his friends and family, he was sentenced to six months hard labour in the State Penitentiary. But he did not have to serve this harsh sentence because, after a dramatic phone call to Coretta King, Senator Kennedy – later President of the USA – managed to set political wheels in motion and Luther King was released.

'Sit-in' demonstrations were extended to 'Freedom Rides'. Pairs of black and white volunteers boarded buses travelling through the south, to test the new law forbidding segregation in bus stations. A great deal of violence resulted, resisting Whites overturning and burning buses and attacking the Freedom Riders. Besides this, riders, including Luther King, were frequently arrested and chose to go to prison rather than pay fines. Soon public attention to the protest became such that non segregation laws were enforced on buses and at bus terminals.

Martin Luther King was next asked to assist in the civil rights struggle in Birmingham, Alabama. He had once described Birmingham as '. . . the most thoroughly segregated city of Alabama', and had said that 'All the evils and injustices the Negro can be subjected to are right there in Birmingham.' Besides this, the Governor of Alabama at that time was George Wallace, whose campaign slogan had been 'Segregation Forever'. The decision by the black population to fight the system and issue a manifesto demanding desegregation was therefore a brave one. The protest began quietly with picketings and 'sit-ins', but an injunction was swiftly passed forbidding demonstrations of any kind. On Good Friday 1963, Luther King deliberately broke the injunction, knowing that he would be gaoled and, with a crowd of supporters, marched through the town. 'All along the way', he wrote, 'Negroes lined the streets. We were singing, and they were joining in. As we neared the town area, Bull Conner – 'the Commissioner of Public Safety' – ordered his men to arrest us'. This time Luther King spent eight days in solitary confinement, where he wrote the famous *Letter from a Birmingham Jail* in which he attempted to answer those critical of his publicity-seeking methods. 'Was not Jesus an extremist for love?' he asked.

After Luther King's release from gaol, the SCLC decided to enlist the schoolchildren of Birmingham in the fight for freedom, since it was the schoolchildren who would benefit most from desegregation, and it was felt that the Freedom Movement would give them a sense of worth and dignity. On 2 May some six thousand schoolchildren marched to demonstrate against school segregation and 959 were arrested. Throughout that week, wave upon wave of children gathered at the Sixteenth Street Baptist Church and marched off singing 'We Shall Overcome' as they went. Bull Connor ordered fire-hoses to be opened on them, and jets of water under a hundred pounds of pressure knocked many children flat, ripping the clothes off some of them. Police dogs were unleashed which ran into the crowds of children, biting and snarling. Tremendous moral indignation built up as the nation viewed pictures of this violence against innocent young people on television. It became imperative to reach a settlement on desegregation. President Kennedy sent a negotiator to Birmingham and, although many white people remained intransigent, an agreement was announced on 10 May in which the principles of desegregation were staked out. White retaliation was immediate: the Klu Klux Klan bombed the home of Luther King's brother and the motel where SCLC members were staying. This enraged the black population and thousands erupted onto the streets. Governor Wallace's National Guard moved in to seal up the black area of the town; but it was Luther King and his friends who stopped the near riot, by travelling all through the area preaching non-violence. Birmingham gradually calmed down; the agreements were implemented and President Kennedy proposed a Civil Rights Bill in 1963 which was eventually passed by Congress in 1964.

Meeting hatred with love, violence with non-violence had worked in the case of Birmingham. The Civil Rights Movement swept on to a climax when, on 27 August, over two hundred and fifty thousand black and white citizens assembled in Washington D.C. for a mass Civil Rights rally. It was here that Luther King delivered his famous 'Let Freedom Ring' address. Moved by the enormous crowd who were calling for him, he abandoned his written speech and spoke from the heart: 'I say to you today, even though we face the difficulties of today and tomorrow, I still have a dream . . . I have a dream that one day this nation will rise up, live out the true meaning of its creed. We hold these truths to be self-evident, that all men are created equal.'

In 1964, the year that the Civil Rights Bill was passed, Luther King received the Nobel Peace Prize. He was continuing to use non-violent means to fight for 'freedom' and, as always, concentrated on the most deeply segregated cities of the South for which to campaign. In 1965 the SCLC chose Selma, Alabama, where only a handful of black citizens had been allowed to vote. A march was planned from Selma to Montgomery to demonstrate the black peoples' determination to vote, but Governor Wallace refused to permit this action. In spite of his prohibition, five hundred people gathered to march on Sunday March 7 but were beaten back by troops who clubbed the crowd, threw tear-gas grenades, and even used electric cattle-prods to force the people to disband. Luther King was horrified but felt that the march must take place. He made a nationwide appeal for people to join in and Selma's black citizens were joined by hundreds of Blacks and Whites from other states, including many notable churchmen. On the following Thursday, over ten thousand people poured out of Selma towards Montgomery but were again halted by troops. This time, to preserve peace, the huge crowd turned back of its own accord, so there was no bloodshed. Eventually, President Johnson, a fervent supporter of Civil Rights, sent in army troops to Alabama so that the demonstrators could march under their protection. And so, on March 21, Luther King marched out of Selma at the head of about five thousand people of all races, and managed to reach Montgomery and continue to Atlanta to present a petition to Governor Wallace.

Next, the SCLC planned to move North and West. 'You can expect us in Baltimore, Philadelphia, Detroit, Los Angeles and Chicago', Luther King said. 'I tell you, we will take the non-violent movement all over the United States.' In 1965 he made a 'people to people' tour of the Northern cities and visited the Watts district of Los Angeles where there had been a devastating eruption of rioting that summer. Although he reaffirmed his own position of non-violence, Luther King understood the intense frustration felt by the black population when their own non-violent tactics left them open to dangerous violence from the opposition, particularly the frustration of Northern and Western Blacks, who lived a ghetto existence but had no obvious villain such as Governor Wallace on which to target their tension. Both he and the SCLC decided to take the Freedom Movement to Chicago, feeling that this city epitomized the despair, hopelessness and desperation of the northern Blacks. He and his family moved to the black ghetto area of Chicago in 1966 and Luther King and his team went about their usual procedure of mass-meetings and demonstrations, including an enormous rally in Soldier Field on Sunday, 10 July 1966. Fifty thousand people came, the meeting was non-violent, but the next day Mayor Daley refused all demands for better conditions for the Blacks. Feelings erupted and rioting broke out all the following night: Luther King became increasingly worried at the violence of this and the other riots and the slowness of achieving desegregation.

At the same time, Martin Luther King became troubled about the American involvement in the war in Vietnam and found himself increasingly pushed towards leadership in anti-war groups. He wrote in a sermon, *Pilgrimage to Nonviolence*, 'I am convinced that the church cannot be silent while mankind faces the threat of nuclear annihilation. If the church is to be true to her mission, she must call for an end to the arms-race'. In 1967, Luther King began speaking directly against the Vietnam War, though many Civil Rights advocates criticized this, thinking that the two issues would become confused.

Martin Luther King continued to campaign for peace at home, as well as international peace. He and other members of the SCLC had long been planning a 'Poor Peoples' Campaign' which would have as its objectives, in Luther King's words, 'Economic security, decent sanitary housing, and quality education for every American'. This time the SCLC was concentrating on the whole nation rather than one city and a 'Poor Peoples' March' was planned which would converge on Washington DC on April 22 1968. Meanwhile, Luther King toured key cities to see at first-hand the plight of the poor and to recruit them for the march. Poor people of all nationalities responded with terrific enthusiasm and the pace of the campaign intensified. To Luther King's wife, Corretta, it seemed now that, 'there were great forces driving him to complete his work . . . the feeling of tremendous urgency he had towards the "Poor Peoples' Campaign" and the preparations that he tried to give his staff, so they could carry on without him, are indications of this' (from *My Life with Martin Luther King Jr*).

Meanwhile, in Memphis, Tennesee, black sanitation workers were striking to protest against unequal pay and poor working-conditions. The protest intensified and spread, with grievances ranging from police brutality to intolerable school conditions and, in March 1968, Luther King felt he must lead the Memphis demonstrations. But the march he led ended in a riot when some frustrated young Blacks began breaking windows, looting and burning shops. Police retaliation was swift and bloody; many people were beaten up and one young man was killed. Martin Luther King was badly upset, but he reiterated his policy of non-violence at a press conference and then, on 3 April in Memphis, addressed a rally and spoke of threats on his own life, urging his followers to continue the non-violent struggle no matter what happened to him. 'Like anybody else', he said, 'I would like to live a long life . . . But I'm not concerned with that now. I just want to do God's will. And He's allowed me to go up to the mountain. And I've looked over, and I've seen the Promised Land. I may not get there with you, but I want you to know tonight that we as a people will get to the Promised Land.'

The next evening, as Luther King stood on an

outside balcony at the Lorraine Hotel, Memphis, he was struck by a rifle bullet. He was pronounced dead at 7.00 p.m. in a Memphis hospital.

Martin Luther King had already prepared himself for death. In a sermon which he preached at the Ebenezer Baptist Church on 4 February 1968, he was specific: '. . . every now and then I think about my own death and I think about my own funeral . . . and I ask myself, "What would I want said?" I'd like somebody to mention that day that . . . "Martin Luther King Jr, tried to give his life serving others" . . . I want you to say . . . that "I tried to be right on the war question", "I did try to feed the hungry". I want you to say that, "I tried to love and serve humanity".'